Campaigns with the 71st Regiment: 1808-14

SEVENTY FIRST REGIMENT.

QUEEN'S COLOUR.

REGIMENTAL COLOUR.

Campaigns with the 71st Regiment: 1808-14

The Recollections of a Private Scottish Soldier During the Peninsular War

ILLUSTRATED

Written by Himself

and

Historical Record of the Seventy-First Regiment Highland Light Infantry (Extract)

Richard Cannon

Campaigns with the 71st Regiment: 1808-14
The Recollections of a Private Scottish Soldier During the Peninsular War
Written by Himself
and
Historical Record of the Seventy-First Regiment Highland Light Infantry (Extract)
by Richard Cannon

ILLUSTRATED

FIRST EDITION IN THIS FORM

First published under the titles
Vicissitudes in the Life of a Scottish Soldier
and
Historical Record of the Seventy-First Regiment Highland Light Infantry (Extract)

Leonaur is an imprint of Oakpast Ltd
Copyright in this form © 2023 Oakpast Ltd

ISBN: 978-1-916535-24-4 (hardcover)
ISBN: 978-1-916535-25-1 (softcover)

http://www.leonaur.com

Publisher's Notes

The views expressed in this book are not necessarily those of the publisher.

Contents

Preface	7
Cork to Mondego Bay	9
A Gallant Action	24
Expedition to Walcheren	42
French Retreat, Our Advance	56
Harassing March to the Field of Albuhera	75
Covering of the Siege of Badajoz	91
Death of Cadogan	106
Brutal Inhumanity	125
A Galling Discovery	144
Historical Record of the Seventy-First Regiment Highland Light Infantry (Extract) *By Richard Cannon*	159

Preface

We possess already many works which present all the grand and general features of our Continental campaigns; but we know very little about the minuter details that gave the Peninsular war its peculiar character and colouring. The courage of our soldiers, their constancy under daily sufferings and privations, their kindness to the foreigners they were protecting, and their generosity to the foe they opposed, have been lauded, in the aggregate, both in prose and in rhyme; but there are few traits preserved of individual prowess and of individual adventure—of the light-heartedness, the misery, the ludicrous or lamentable incidents, the vices and the virtues that diversify the life and character of a private soldier.

The single subject here selected for a picture will, in the main points, illustrate the personal condition of the whole of our army; and, from such a story, many particulars may be learned regarding the conduct of the officers engaged in the Peninsular war, which could in no other way be obtained; for the commanders would hardly be vain enough to chronicle their own acts of generosity,—and they might be withheld by shame, and their historians by delicacy, from speaking of the deeds of despotism and cruelty in which it is known that some of them have occasionally indulged.

On these accounts, therefore, the *Vicissitudes in the Life* of our Scottish Soldier will, no doubt, be perused with interest—an interest which will, by no means be diminished by the publication of the fact, that he belonged to the 71st regiment—one of the most gallant in the service, and one from which there has already emanated a similar narrative, which has excited no small portion of public attention and applause.

Chapter 1

Cork to Mondego Bay

The reader of this work can have little interest in knowing my name, and therefore I have suppressed it altogether. It is sufficient to say, that I was born in the city of Glasgow; enlisted at the age of sixteen; passed through the usual routine of a soldier's life in the three kingdoms; and, after having been in more than one corps, I eventually entered the 71st, or Glasgow regiment, when it had just arrived from South America. The very name of this corps, and its containing so many of my townsmen and acquaintances, will account for my desire to belong to it.

In the year 1808 we were lying at Cork along with the army forming there under the command of Sir Arthur Wellesley. It was on the 5th of June that we embarked, totally ignorant of the place of our destination. It is true, there were many surmises afloat, such as, that we were going to America, and so forth: but, after all, we lay snug in the Cove of Cork for about five weeks; during the whole of which time, the deck of the vessel that I was in, was a continual scene of uproar and jovial mirth. Every afternoon the piper played his best reel-tunes, to which the men danced in high glee; liquor was also very plentifully handed about.

This was chiefly owing to the settlement of a long arrear of pay due to the soldiers, who had arrived from America. Our vessel, the *Plantagenet*, belonged to Kirkcaldy, or, at any rate, the crew were all natives of that place. They had, like other Scotch vessels, always a liberal allowance of kale: their old greasy cook, like the rest of his trade, being fonder of drink than of meat, was constantly going about the deck, offering to "gie a ladlefu' o' kail for a drappy o' drink." One day we were ordered ashore to be inspected; the small boat that I was in being leaky, one of our men (a Highlander) thinking, it seems, to rectify this defect, suddenly pulled a plug out, and the water, of course, rushed in upon us in great quantities.

The author of this misfortune had not the presence of mind which one of his countrymen had when in a similar predicament; this was, to thrust his thumb into the hole and cut it off. Fortunately, we were near the shore, or the most tragical consequences might have taken place. On questioning the Highlandman, his only excuse was, "that he thought to let the water out!"

At length, on the 12th of July, the fleet put out to sea; it consisted of seventy transports, two men of war, and a gunbrig, the whole containing about 10,000 troops. While the land was receding from our view, every deck was covered by the men taking a last look at Ireland. At a time like this, when one's country is diminishing into a speck upon the waters, even the most careless are thoughtful. An ordinary passenger has only the dangers of the sea and climate to fear; but the soldier has, in addition, those of war; he feels a certainty that, among the numbers around him, many will never return,—"and who knows," he thinks to himself, "but I may be one of them?"

But our reflections soon began to be sadly disturbed; present misery alone engrossed the attention of all; for a stiff though favourable breeze had sprung up, which in a short time threw nearly the whole of our men into the pains of sea-sickness. Out of 250 on board, perhaps there were not above a dozen of us that could stand upright, or, in other words, were well. Happily, for me, I was among the latter number: in fact, I have never felt this complaint in the slightest degree, and was, of course, a little surprised to see many in a pitiable state who had even twice crossed the line.

In a *gourmand's* eyes, I was a happy man that day; the mess I belonged to consisted of six men, but as they were all sick except myself, the whole of their provisions and rum fell to my share;

and the value of this was considerably enhanced on account of its being pudding-day.

Nothing particular occurred during the rest of the voyage. We passed swiftly through the Bay of Biscay, saw Cape Finisterre in Spain; and, after a passage of fourteen days, our fleet dropped their anchors in Mondego Bay. We rode at anchor for some days, during which time a heavy swell prevailed through the bay, which made the vessels pitch and roll in a very disagreeable manner. The difficulty of walking on the deck was increased by the old cook's slush, or grease barrel, being overturned by accident. Previous to our landing, everyone was busily engaged in cleaning himself from the dirt inseparable from a crowded transport. The morning of the 3rd of August saw us in the boats, leaving the old *Plantagenet* without a tear.

As we approached the beach, crowds of Portuguese welcomed us by repeated acclamations; and no sooner had we leaped on the peninsular shore, than a number of women came down, and distributed fruit among us in great abundance: each of them had her apron loaded. Having nothing ready to put the fruit in, I took off my bonnet; scarcely had I done so, when it was filled to the head—legions of hands striving with one another to get something in. After remaining a short time on the beach, we crossed the River Mondego in Portuguese boats, and then commenced our march.

Here, for the first time I believe, the shores of Portugal resounded with the yell of a Scottish bagpipe. A foretaste of campaigning miseries now began; the day was insufferably hot; no water could be had; our fatigue and thirst were also increased by being obliged to wade through the burning sands of the coast. Two leagues had been gone over, when the order to halt was given. Rejoiced at the, news, I threw myself under the shade of a tree, and soon fell into a comfortable nap. On awakening, I found myself in a tented field, a number of the men having been employed in erecting a canvass city. We remained some days encamped, waiting, till the stores were landed.

On the 10th we advanced up the country: on the 14th the

advanced guard of our army had a skirmish with the French. In the course of this march, we began to get rather sceptical in our belief of the Portuguese being so overjoyed and grateful for the interference of the British. As we were passing through the village of Alcobaca, an old blind woman stood on a hillock, bawling, with all her might, "*Viva los Françesos!*"

On hearing this, another woman went up, and whispered something into her ear; instantly she began to call out, as lustily as before, "*Viva los Ingles!*" She evidently had taken us for Frenchmen, till warned of the mistake; but the adulation was then too common, or rather late for us to swallow. Perhaps the sentiments of the whole nation, with regard to us, might have been gained from this old lady: armed foreigners, although they have friendly intentions, are always distrusted.

It was not till the 16th that I first beheld the French; they were posted on the heights of Roleia. Here I could not but reflect, that these men are what is called our "hereditary enemies." How false is that name! what quarrel had we with that party of men opposite us? what injury had they done us? They had unjustly subdued the Portuguese—but that was no business of ours. To give liberty to an oppressed nation, we were come; yes, this is the most plausible pretext for murder.

But to the point. Preparations were now made to drive the enemy from their situation; part of our army advanced to the attack, the light company only of our regiment accompanied the attacking party. I was, with the rest of the regiment, stationary. The engagement now commenced, but we could only see at a distance the "tug of war."

The incessant discharge of musquetry, and the smoke and loud roar of artillery, completed the effect: occasionally, however, a stray cannon-ball from the French would whistle over our heads, and sink with a heavy sound, into the earth. One of these formidable missiles struck off an artilleryman's leg, close by us. This was sufficient to remind us, that even where we were, safety was out of the question.

The most part of the day we were tormented with thirst,

although there was no want of springs around us. The reason of this was, that some of our men, while hot and fatigued, had drunk the water, which naturally causing, in their state, a disagreeable effect, reports were immediately spread, that the French had poisoned the water. We were then young enough warriors to believe this, and consequently did not dare to touch a drop.

The enemy having commenced a retreat, we were ordered to advance. While marching up a road, I passed over the dead body of a young Swiss soldier, his red clothing enabling us to know his nation.

He had received a ball in the middle of the forehead. This was the first victim to the deity of war I had yet seen, but, as we advanced, many more met our sight. The road and contiguous fields were literally covered with dead and dying, both British and French. The horror of the scene was much increased in consequence of the hedges and long grass taking fire. We had to endure the appalling view of the impotent efforts of several poor wounded wretches endeavouring to drag themselves from the devouring flames: there was no time to render them assistance; besides, self-preservation warned us that danger was to be apprehended from the fire communicating with our cartridge-boxes. After reaching the summit of the heights, there was nothing to do but to look at the French filing off in columns.

Thus concluded the Battle of Roleia. The French were only 6,000 strong: our army was much superior in number, although not all engaged. Upon the whole, therefore, there was no great reason for us to boast. We gained our point by compelling the enemy to quit the heights; but they effected this in good order.

Next morning, we marched to the village of Vimiera, and encamped, in its environs for two days. Here the army was joined by reinforcements under General Anstruther; they had landed in Peniche Bay.

The 21st of August, 1808, was destined to be a memorable day—at least so far as the death of thousands could make it so. It was Sunday; we had been ordered to attend divine service in

The 71st at the Battle of Vimiero

the morning, and were accordingly preparing ourselves for this, when the drum of the 40th regiment beating to arms, gave a general alarm. On hearing the bruit, Colonel Pack came out of his tent and ordered us to fall in, as the enemy were advancing to the attack. We then marched, and took up a position on a rising ground in the left of our army; thus, contrary to expectation, we found ourselves about to enter into a service totally different to that which was at first intended.

The battle had by this time commenced on the right; consequently, as at Roleia. We were obliged to stand for a while exposed to a distant cannonade. A shell also fell and burst near our company; one of the splinters wounded a man severely, who stood the third from me on the left. A party of officers went out at one time, a short distance from us, in order to obtain a closer view of the engagement; one of them, belonging to the 82nd, fell dead in our sight; slain, strange to say, by the mere wind of a cannon-ball; not a scratch being on his body. The balls were, now flying so thick, that we received orders to sit down: even in this position, they would ever and *anon* rattle through among the fixed bayonets, and descend so low as to knock the bonnets off our heads!

We remained in this tantalising state for some time, really envying our comrades on the right, who had an opportunity of revenging themselves; truly the situation we were then placed in is the most trying' for the soldier's courage. He feels in himself an indescribable terror, which is entirely unknown when once he has fairly entered the hottest part of an engagement.

At length we beheld, with great satisfaction, the enemy advancing towards us. We then stood to our arms, our flank files ran out to skirmish, but they were soon driven in again by the steady approach of the French. I had now an opportunity to see them face to face; they differed widely from us in dress in this instance, being all clothed in long white smock-frocks and trowsers, and having hairy knapsacks hanging loosely on their backs.

But little time was left for observation, on account of General

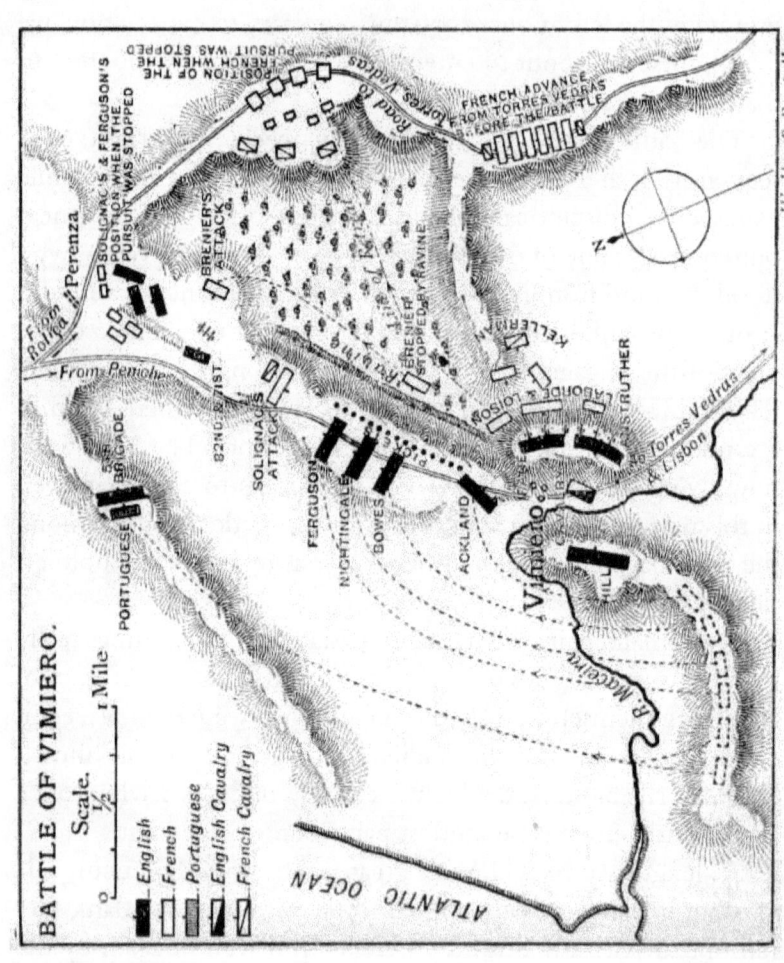

Ferguson riding up to the —th, which lay close beside us, and ordering that regiment to charge; but, for what cause I never could learn, the whole regiment remained motionless. Colonel, Pack, on seeing this, went to the general, and requested permission for us to advance in their stead: and this being granted at once, we, along with the 36th and 82nd regiments, instantly rushed forward, and fired a tremendous volley, which we saw did great execution.

The astonished enemy, on getting such a warm reception, fell into confusion, and began to retrograde; this encouraging us, we gave three hearty cheers, and pressed on: our grenadier company, and the 36th light company, charged with the bayonet, and took six pieces of cannon. We still advanced, and two other pieces of cannon fell into our hands, the enemy not having time to hurry them across a ravine which lay in the way: meanwhile, the enemy continued his retreat, and soon disappeared over an eminence.

A remarkable instance of the presentiment of death occurred during the early part of the day. While we were marching to join the rest of the army, one of our men, named Sweeny, an Irishman, happened, somehow or other, to get out of his place in the ranks. An officer observed this, and threatened to punish him for his fault. The spirit of this unhappy man had appeared for some time back to be broken, in consequence of frequent reprimands, yet he never was guilty of any heinous crime; he seemed, in short, to have been what is called "born under an unlucky star," never pleasing his commanders. The last act of power had weighed so heavy on his mind, that he was heard to say, "I will give no more offence:" something more was overheard, tending to express the poor fellow's confidence of a speedy dissolution.

The words were truly prophetic, for, in less than half an hour afterwards, he was shot dead. I have often heard and read of similar occurrences, but could never account for them: can it be the soul that feels the approach of danger, and warns the grosser senses? or can it be mere chance? If the latter, how comes it that death is the never-failing consequence, when the men have solemnly assured their incredulous comrades of their internal forebodings? But, after all, I am not so enthusiastic in this belief as to deny that there may have been many who were confident of meeting their death in battle, and yet have escaped safe and sound; but of this kind of persons I never knew one.

Another of our men had his bonnet driven off his head, and set on fire, by a shell; but he never stopt an instant to reflect on his miraculous escape, for, snatching up the unfortunate Sweeny's bonnet, he clapt it on his head with great *sang froid*, although it (the bonnet) contained some of the blood and brains of its former possessor.

In going over the bloody field, a French general (Bernier) was discovered lying wounded; his horse had been shot under him: his *aide-de-camp*, and an orderly dragoon had been endeavouring to extricate him, without effect. They therefore chose to remain faithfully by their master, and were accordingly taken along with him. The appearance of the *aide-de-camp* was shocking; he had been wounded about the mouth, which occasioned such a flow of blood as to dye his breast and white trowsers quite scarlet. This officer's horse, a beautiful Arabian, was seized as a lawful prize by one of our men; but Colonel Pack deprived him of it, on account of his well-known intemperate habits.

The story of Corporal Mackay capturing General Bernier, and magnanimously refusing the proffered presents, has often been written and spoken of: the real truth of the matter was this:—An Irish lad, named Gaven, was the first that espied the general, and without hesitation he made him prisoner, exclaiming, at the same time, "By Jasus! I have taken the sarjant-major of the French." Just at that time Mackay came up, and took him out of Gaven's hands; and then it was that the watch and purse were offered, and refused—Mackay knowing well that it would be too barefaced a trick to take what should have belonged to another, particularly when there were so many witnesses to the transaction. What was the sequel of this?

The pawky corporal received a gold medal from the Highland Society, and his name was highly lauded in every *Gazette*;

finally, I believe, he received a commission! If there was any merit in the thing, poor Gaven should have had it; yet he never received either honour or reward. What was the cause of this injustice, is a natural question? I blush to answer: it was because Mackay was a Scotchman, and, furthermore, a Highlander; the latter particular was an infallible recommendation to a set of old drivellers, who lay, and still lie, constantly on the watch, to hunt out and blaze forth to the world anything tending to distinguish the Highland name—sometimes in despite of truth.

I am not yet done with this general, or at least with his sword. It was strange, but true, that this sword was destined to occasion both trouble and danger, not only to me, but to the whole of the company to which I belonged. The sword had fallen into the possession of one of the men, who afterwards presented it to our captain, who unfortunately thought proper to wear it. This did not escape the notice of the colonel, who immediately forbade him from carrying it longer. Ever after this, our worthy colonel had an antipathy to the company, as if we were all to blame in this paltry affair. "We could do nothing right" after this; and on one occasion the whole company was ordered out to the field, when only twelve men out of each of the other companies were sent. Perhaps some may think that this was an honour, instead of a punishment, to us; but at that disastrous time (the period of the Retreat from Corunna), fatigue and misery quelled every idea of glory:—but more of this hereafter.

I return to the principal subject. While several of us were around General Bernier, the French orderly dragoon, who had remained by him, thought proper to clap spurs to his horse, and set off at full speed. Astonished at this, we stood looking at the rapid flight of our supposed prisoner; but soon recollecting ourselves, a shower of bullets was sent after him, and I fully believe a hundred musquets were discharged without effect. His temerity was successful; he escaped over the hill. After the armistice, I saw this man in our camp, and heard him laughing at his own *ruse de guerre*. While we were resting on our arms, a body of cavalry was suffered to approach us, under the idea that they were

Portuguese but on our discovering them to be French, by their preparations to fall upon us, we made ready to receive them in no friendly manner: on observing this, they thought proper, to make a precipitate retreat. The French and Portuguese cavalry were then so much alike in appearance, that the latter had taken the precaution to tie white strings round their arms, in order to prevent mistakes; but the French had artfully done the same thing.

The day being oppressively hot, we had piled arms, erroneously concluding that our labours were over, at least for the day; we were accordingly refreshing ourselves, by drinking water, and making frequent attacks on the grapes in a vineyard, when the advance of the French a second time was announced, by the clang of trumpets and beating of drums—which latter action, as it appeared, was much easier performed than the beating of us. We soon caught up our arms, and retired to a short distance. By this time the enemy were within ken; but immediately on our giving them another astounding and destructive volley, they put about, and ran up the hill with surprising speed. We ascended the hill, in pursuit of them; but on arriving at the top, we found that victory had declared decidedly for the British. Thus ended the Battle of Vimiera.

We were much amused while resting from our gory toil, by seeing one of our men taking the remains of a shirt off his back, and then drawing on a dead Frenchman's smock-frock in its stead—his own shirt, it seems, being in anything but good condition. Sir Arthur Wellesley now came up, and passed some very high encomiums on us; and well he might, for there is certainly little vanity in asserting that the 71st contributed in no small degree to the success of this eventful day; a melancholy proof of this is the fact that we had 119 killed and wounded in our regiment alone.

Some may think that I have not given a general account of the Battle of Vimiera; perhaps in this they are right—but how can a private soldier pretend to see a whole engagement? The thing will be plainly seen to be utterly impossible, when it is considered, that the length of a stone's cast is often the extent of his view, while the conflict sometimes extends over miles. Such being the case, I will confine myself chiefly to what came under my own immediate observation; which I dare say will satisfy the reader better than if I had made up my narrative from gazettes, or stolen from others.

The conclusion of this campaign in Portugal is well known, and displayed an additional proof of the ill effects of allowing British commanders to become cabinet ministers. A foolish armistice was entered into by Wellesley and others by which the French were allowed to evacuate the country, loaded with the plunder of the Portuguese: but as I had, to use a vulgar expression, as little to do with the armistice as the man in the moon, I shall here pass it over.

After the Battle of Vimiera; we marched to Torres Vedras, and from thence to the banks of the Tagus: here we saw ten Russian men-of-war at anchor. The whole of this delightful march was extremely pleasant, every spot being in the highest state of cultivation, the climate fine, the face of the country beautiful, in short, differing widely, in all respects, from the bleak glens of Scotland. We continued to wend our way along the edge of the majestic Tagus for six or seven miles, till the city of Lisbon rose on our view.

This sight was grand beyond description; but we afterwards found that the often-repeated accounts of its filthy interior and beautiful exterior, were perfectly correct, it being exactly similar, in this respect, to what we have heard of Constantinople and other Mediterranean cities. We entered and encamped in the Queen's Park, a large green in the vicinity of Lisbon, the French being at that time quartered in the city. No sooner had we pitched our tents, than immense crowds of the citizens came out to see us, of all ranks: Colonel Pack, wishing to amuse them, ordered the band to play.

I happening to be posted to keep the people from incommoding the musicians, was accosted by a fat priest, in good English, who inquired if there were any Lincolnshire men in our regiment? I was unable to give him any information on this point. I said that there were few Englishmen among us; that we were mostly Scotchmen. He then told me that he was an Englishman himself—thus accounting for his knowledge of our language. The good-humoured priest on parting offered me some money, which I refused.

Next day new tartan trowsers were served out, our old ones being in a miserably tattered state, owing to the effects of our campaign. They were now thrown away: this produced a fearful scuffle among some of the lower orders of Portuguese, every one of them contending, with the utmost noise and fury, for the possession of a pair of breeks: to, their honour it must be said, however, or rather to free them, in some degree, from the national reproach, I must say, that, when it was discovered that the clothes were filled with myriads of those disgusting insects which are usual companions of poverty and campaigning, they threw the rags down with every sign of aversion.

Perhaps it is necessary here to apologise or account for our seeming uncleanliness; this is an easy task. Figure to yourself, reader, men landing from a crowded transport without receiving the luxury of clean linen, marching and bivouacking for weeks together without ever putting off their clothes; and your wonder will then cease.

One day a party of our men was sent down to protect, the embarkation of some sick and wounded French from the ruthless violence of a Portuguese mob. During the whole of our stay in the park, the city was illuminated every night, on account, I presume, of the expulsion of the Gallic invaders. The ostrich feathers on our Highland bonnets had become so much the admiration of the Portuguese ladies, that no less than a dollar was offered for each of them by the hawkers about the camp; and this induced some villains amongst us to rob their comrades. I suffered in this way, in common with some others, having my bonnet completely plucked while I was asleep. Instead, of receiving even commiseration for my loss; I was compelled to pay 2*l*. sterling for a new bonnet; and was in danger of being flogged besides: such is military justice!

Several deserters came over here from the French Army to the British. They were of different nations, Swiss, Germans, and Italians; nearly the whole of them, about twenty in number, chose to enlist in out regiment, I know not for what, reason, (as every corps in our army was open to them,) unless the wearing of tartan was considered as a fine thing by these mercenary fellows. It was a common saying among us, that they could serve three kings with one pair of shoes! One of the Italians was possessed of Herculean strength; he would sometimes carry a log of wood which three of us could scarcely move!

CHAPTER 2

A Gallant Action

The month of October had, arrived, when we were roused from our repose, by receiving orders to advance into Spain. The beginning of winter was no auspicious time to commence our deplorable march, but of course we could only murmur secretly at the unwelcome news, and prepare to meet the worst.

Sir John Moore had now superseded Wellesley in the command of the army, the whole of which was broken up into several divisions, which were to take different routes, but all to rendezvous about Salamanca. Sir John Hope being intrusted with the command of a division, consisting of the 71st, 2nd, 36th, and 92nd regiments, as well as the artillery of the army, we all moved off from Lisbon, and marched along the side of the Tagus; we then crossed the river at Abrantes.

I was billeted that night, along, with some others, upon an old Portuguese woman. We were, however, in danger of being expelled from her house, through the levity of one of our men. Seeing that the chimney piece was covered with small images of saints, he inquired their names, with an affected air of gravity; the old woman answered his questions with great-politeness, until, laying his hand upon one, he told her, that he knew very well this was the figure of the *Diablo*. Horrified at the supposed impiety of the remark, she ran out of the house mumbling imprecations on our heads. We were somewhat alarmed soon after, by an officer entering the place; he had been sent by Colonel Pack to inquire into the matter—for it seems she had run open-mouthed to complain to him of the "blasphemous heretics" however, the officer, seeing the thing in its proper light, quietly went away.

Passing through Porto Ligero, we arrived at Campo Mayor, where we lay for a fortnight in an old battery. Bidding *adieu* to the kingdom of Portugal for a while, we continued our march to Badajoz, a frontier town of Spain. A number of the citizens of that place were in waiting for our arrival, and welcomed us with loud acclamations.

After lying ten days in the barracks of Badajoz, we started again, passed through Merida, the capital of Estremadura; from thence we trudged on through Truxillo, famous for being the birthplace of Pizarro, the conqueror of Peru; then crossed the Tagus again at Almaraz, passed through Talavera, well known as the scene of a bloody battle between the French and British, not, long after this period. Continuing our march, we arrived at the town of Escurial, having, at one time, approached so near to Madrid, that we could plainly distinguish its spires.

In the course of this march, we had not the opportunities of knowing the manners and customs of the inhabitants, which we afterwards had; however, we could not, but see something of them, even hurried as our journey was. The character of the men, was as yet incomprehensible to us, excepting that we saw they considered us as uninvited intruders: as for the women, much could not be said for their, virtue.

When we entered Spanish towns, we invariably found crowds of the people receiving us with the most hospitable looks, and bawling loudly the kindest wishes for our long life, and so forth: but when our billets were served out, and we had gone to the places designated in them, the doors were always fast, and the "*viva*" people nowhere to be seen; and if we chanced to find any of the neighbours, we were told that the inmates of the house were from home. Finding that they were attempting to "humbug" us, we henceforth laid down a system which always produced the desired effect: this was, to commence an attack on the billeted doors with the but-ends of our musquets: no sooner had we begun this, than the women of the houses were seen running towards us, holding up their keys, to shew that the doors were now to be opened. It was in this manner that we at length generally obtained admission.

Warned by experience, our men, instead of receiving the congratulations of the Spaniards at the ends of towns with complacency, only answered them with curses; being well aware, that the loudest of the hollow well-wishers would be the first to become invisible when the night's quarters were in the case. After all, the poor devils could not be blamed, considering that they had been already so much harassed and worried by the French Armies. It is true that we came as friends; but it is well known, even in our own country, what inconveniences billeted soldiers occasion to a poor family.

When we were once housed, the Spaniards were very liberal in their *offers* of meat, but it was evidently with the expectation of our refusal; their oil and garlic being still detestable to us. Their fireplaces were generally hung round with fine sausages, of which, I believe, it would not have required great eloquence to make us accept; but we seldom or, never got the offer, I presume for this very reason. The wary people invariably sat up all night when we were in their houses, and watched us, as we lay on the floor, with the eyes of lynxes: they had, indeed, some reason, as several attempts were made to pilfer their sausages; but in this we were seldom successful, a little salt, being in general the amount of our thefts. That article hung in a box near the fireplace, exactly similar to what is usual in the common houses of Scotland.

I mentioned our arrival at Escurial before. This town is remarkable for containing a palace of the kings of Spain, which is said to be the largest building in Europe. I went down one day to see this place, along with two of our men, and meeting a priest by the way, he politely took us into the palace, and after shewing us part of it, he led us into his own apartment, where we found two other priests. These jovial fellows soon produced some case-bottles of generous wine and plenty of cigars, which the whole of us fell upon with great good will, and we became as friendly as if we had been acquainted with one another for many years.

However, it was only one of the three Scotchmen of the party that could talk Spanish well; he had been in South America, consequently the priests and he kept up what, I presume, was a very interesting conversation about that country: but as I and my comrade could understand little or nothing of this, we sat silently quaffing our wine and smoking with "tranquil delight."

I felt it strange to be sitting in such a friendly manner with Spanish-Catholic priests—men whom, I had so often heard represented as a sort of demi-devils; who, no, doubt, had in the same way considered us in a similar light. When will religious prejudice completely disappear from the face of the earth, as it did, (at least to appearance) in one humble case?

Another day, a party of officers and men having gone to see the palace, I, went a second time. On entering, I found the party coming out of the Pantheon, or tombs of the Spanish monarchs. I therefore, lost this sight, but was abundantly compensated by seeing the rest of this superb place.

Certainly, I had no, idea that such grandeur existed; one of the numerous halls exceeded any of the rest in this respect; its floor was beautifully chequered with black and white marble; it contained also a magnificent altar, with statues of Christ and the Virgin Mary, of Solid gold! There were a number of courts throughout the place, each containing a *jet d'eau*, and a fountain filled with goldfish. The walls of every apartment and lobby were covered with paintings; but being no connoisseur in the arts, I cannot descant upon the respective merits of their painter; all that I will venture to say is, that they pleased me highly. The subjects were chiefly sacred—views of purgatory, and representations of miracles; portraits of apostles, saints, sinners, priests, and devils.

In all parts of the palace figures of gridirons are to be seen; indeed, the building itself is in that form, out of respect to the martyrdom of St. Lawrence, who, it seems, was roasted to death on one of those instruments. This huge monument of bigotry and profusion was built at an expense of 3,300,000 pounds, by Philip the Second, in consequence of the success of his prayer that he might gain a victory over the French. The palace contains a pantheon, a church, and a convent; 4,000 windows and 8,000 doors; 3,000 priests were lodged and fed there when we visited it first, not one of whom remained the next time we entered the country.

But our short dream of pleasure was again disturbed by the issuing of an order to march. This word strongly reminded us that we were not travelling either for instruction or amusement, that we had no will of our own; and, in short, that we were slaves, that must kill or be killed, or starve, or perish with cold, or walk to the end of the world if commanded.

Leaving the Escurial, after a stay of five days, we crossed a pass in a chain of mountains, and continued our march to join the main body of the British Army. One night I was billeted, along with some others, in a house where we were shewn into a miserable dog-hole of an apartment; seeing better rooms in the place, we used the military freedom of removing, and taking possession of one of them. This act drew upon us the ire of the inhabitants, and we were assailed with a dreadful storm of oaths and imprecations.

One of our men, the best Spanish scholar among us, instantly, arose and attacked them in turn with their own weapons, pouring out volleys of the bitterest words he could devise: to our astonishment, this, instead of adding fuel to the flame, produced an immediate reconciliation, and the greatest harmony reigned among us during the remainder of our stay.

One of our officers having got possession of a pony, thought proper to mount it while upon the march next day. No doubt it was his intention to ease his aching feet; but being a very, unsightly, rider, and no favourite in the regiment to boot, we now saw our opportunity, and embraced it: a shout of derision burst simultaneously from every lip, the noise of which alarmed the pony so much that it went off at full speed. Our hero apparently, had not calculated upon such a "show off;" for he exclaimed, in tremulous accents, "Oh, what a fall I shall get!"

Horror was visibly depicted on his countenance; however, he grasped the saddle firmly, and continued to roar manfully for help; but this no person seemed in a hurry to afford; on the contrary, the whole, regiment was convulsed, with laughter, to see their arch-enemy for once in such a disgraceful situation—even the officers joined in the laugh. The whole concluded with the unfortunate horseman's overthrow, with, however, very little damage to himself, as he soon got up, uttering curses, "not loud, but deep." For a long time after this he was pretty well humbled by his fall.

Intelligence having arrived of the rapid advance of the French towards Madrid, our division hastened to overtake Moore's army. In our bivouac that night we took great precautions, forming a square about ourselves with the guns, in order to prevent a surprise. Next morning, in passing through a village, the inhabitants brought out several casks of *aguardiente* to the roadside, and treated every man of us as we marched by. At length we arrived at Alva de Tormes, where it began to be whispered, that the French were pouring into Spain in such numbers that we must soon be driven out of the country. Hurrying on, we now joined the main body of our army near Salamanca.

We had some diversion on the road with the hypocrisy of two fellows: one of them, it appears, had stolen a hen and deposited it in his: haversack; but being unaware that there was a hole in it, the hen's head came out and hung dangling in the sight of every person in his rear. His comrades, with the intention of quizzing him, brought on the subject of pilfering from the Spaniards, and every now and then one would give a pull at the head, till at last almost the whole of the fowl was exposed to view. Meanwhile the man trudged on, totally unconscious of our sport, and joining heartily in uttering the bitterest invectives against those who would rob the poor inhabitants. In due time he was warned of what was behind him; and it may easily be conceived what his looks and sensations were in consequence.

The other fellow's case was something of a similar nature. We all knew that his haversack was filled with stolen sausages, a dog having followed at his heels for, a whole day. The same trick, was played again; the hypocrite professed also to have a mortal detestation of all plunderers; he was accordingly justly exposed to derision.

About this time it fell to my lot to be appointed one of the commissary's guards (twelve in number); that is to say, I had to guard the waggons of provisions and wine. Although this job had the appearance of being good, I found it totally the reverse, having far harder service to perform than if I had been along with the regiment; the lazy waggons being constantly in the rear of a retreating army, and thereby more exposed to the attacks of the enemy's advanced parties. The first night of my being on guard it was so dreadfully cold, that I could not even taste some wine which an artilleryman offered me: some of my comrades, it appears, could drink well enough, however—for a pigskin of liquor was stolen from the waggons in the course of the night.

The commissary was very wroth on discovering his loss; he menaced us with a court martial, of which the slight punishment of hanging was to be the result. We continued crawling along the road at a snail's pace, when we came upon the way with a soldier's wife and three wretched children, who had fallen behind the army; they were accommodated in our waggons; at length we arrived at a village, when it was getting dark. Our commissary, wishing to see the *alcalde* of the place, alighted, and, tying his horse to a gate, went to look for him.

When the *alcalde* was found, after a long search, the commissary went to untie his horse, but found that some of the honest villagers had saved him that trouble, there being no trace of the animal to be seen. The enraged commissary, maddened at his repeated losses, began to storm and swear in the most horrible manner; but bethinking himself that this vapouring would not bring back his steed, he made a bold attempt to play off a *ruse de guerre, à la* Captain Cook:—seizing the *alcalde*, he told him that he was a prisoner until the horse was brought back. But this would not do—the worthy *alcalde* laughed him to scorn; so that he had to suffer the misfortune quietly.

No corner being now left in his heart for pity, we were ordered to move on to Sahagun, although it was three leagues distant, and the night pitch dark. A hundred yards had scarcely been gone over, when we were obliged to halt, in consequence of the frost being intense, and the waggon mules unshod. Never shall I forget that dreadful night, through the whole of which I had to stand in the street of this inhospitable village, where no shelter was to be had. I was so benumbed with cold, and oppressed with sleep, that I fell several times to the ground, in spite of my endeavours to remain upright, by leaning on my musquet.

Meanwhile the muleteers were snug in the waggons: one of them handed out some wine to me, on condition that I was to take charge of two spare mules till the morning. But I had not the beasts long under my surveillance—for the commissary came up with one of our men and a Spanish guide, and ordered them to take the mules and ride forward to Sahagun, to inform General Moore of the cause of our delay. Not daring to resist this command, I reluctantly surrendered my trust. Daylight at length appeared, and the rays of the sun soon began to melt the frost; this enabled us to move on, and at last we reached Sahagun.

The poor muleteer, on missing his mules, inquired very anxiously of me about them; and on my informing him, as well as I could, of the particulars, he shook his head, as much as to say, that they were for ever lost. His suspicions were verified; for after the commission had been delivered, the rascally guide, having heed intrusted to take back the mules, seized the opportunity of making off with them, never to return.

I now quitted with pleasure the old crusty commissary's service, and joined my regiment. We lay in Sahagun for some days. One evening we were turned out suddenly about six o'clock, and told to have our flints in good order—but, after all, nothing of moment was done, though we stood, till twelve o'clock at night, cooling our heels in the streets, and then marched about a mile out of the town; but the intenseness of the frost still impeded the progress of the artillery so much, that we were forced to return to our old quarters.

We marched on to Benevente. About this time some of our parties had a skirmish with the French, and several prisoners were brought in, among whom was General Lefevre. We continued our disastrous retreat, for it could now only be so called, the French pursuing us sharply, in mighty numbers. The roads began now to be in a terrible state, in consequence of a continual rain; the mud rose as high as our knees; and this destroyed all appearance of order in the march, every one trying to pick his way in the best manner he could. As far as the eye could reach, our army had the resemblance of a straggling flock of drenched ducks, rather than of bold warriors.

Wading like the rest, very dolefully along, I stept upon a seemingly smooth and dry part of the road; and before I knew where I was, I found myself up to the middle in mud. The mud was so tough, that, in spite of every effort to extricate myself, I stuck fast for a considerable time, during which no endeavours were made to assist me, everyone being too busily engaged with his own misfortunes to mind those of others.

Having succeeded, at length, in getting out of the slough, although at the expense of a pair of shoes, I made shift to get up to the regiment. Arriving at a village, we obtained quarters. Being much in want of a pair of good shoes, a thought came into my head (God forgive me) of possessing myself of a stout pair, belonging to my Spanish landlord. They lay very temptingly in view; but considering that if I was to cram them at once into my haversack, they might be missed before I could get out of the house, and being unwilling to abide the disagreeable consequences of this, I hit upon a seemingly better scheme, of covering them; as it were by chance, with my knapsack and accoutrements.

I lay till morning in full expectation of possessing the prize, but my plan was completely defeated by the old Spaniard's rising early, and commencing a search for his brogues. I lay still, knowing well what he was looking for, hugging myself with the idea that the scheme was so laid, that if they were discovered no blame could be attached to anyone. At length the old *don*, in turning over everything, perceived the identical shoes, and "grinning horribly a ghastly smile,"—he lugged them triumphantly forth; and went away without saying anything.

Next morning, continuing our wade, we arrived at a river; and forded it. An officer, before crossing, ordered one of the men to carry him over but just as he had mounted the man's back, Colonel Pack observed the transaction, and immediately ordered the delicate gentleman to be set down, and to ford the water himself. After passing through the towns of Astorga and Villa Franca, we began the ascent of an exceeding high mountain, on the first day of the year 1809; The want of provisions was now seriously felt; and this, united to the fatigue, caused many to fall, never to rise again.

In ransacking a village which we came to, some potatoes and honey were found; this allayed the pain of our gnawing stomachs a little: scarcely any of us slept during the whole night, the cooking of the potatoes engrossing almost all our attention. We then marched to the town of Lugo, where we remained one night and part of a day; but the enemy being just at our heels, it was not thought prudent to stay longer; we were therefore obliged to evacuate the town, and bivouac on its outside, with heavy hearts. It was, indeed, a miserable night: thrust out to the storm, and the rain lashing on me in torrents, I threw myself down in the mud, on the lee side of a stone dyke, as the best shelter I could find. Certainly, there was no respect of persons here: the elements are remarkably impartial in such cases as these; and on looking round the field I saw Colonel Pack squatting close by my side.

The French had been long hanging on our rear like a cloud, which now, however, seemed as if it were about to burst—as on the morning of the next day they attacked us in earnest; twelve men out of each of the other companies, and the whole of ours, were sent out to stem their way. I was among the party that was placed as a reserve: in this situation the enemy began peppering us with cannon-balls, upon which we had recourse to our old system of sitting down. Happening to be under a tree, it was struck several times, and the man who sat next me got his musquet broke to splinters in his hand, without receiving the slightest injury; the same ball, after forcing its way through a stone wall, continued its course to the very lines. Darkness put an end to the skirmish, in which an odd incident had occurred. One of the men actually brought in a French prisoner *hooked by the cheek with his fixed bayonet.* To prevent mistakes, it is necessary to mention, that this was not done with any cruel intention, but in the mere, hurry of the moment.

Grim hunger was again preying on our vitals, without any prospect of our driving him out; when one of our company fortunately got hold of a bullock, which it appears had made its escape from the French. The poor animal apparently did not better its condition by desertion, as the time was but short before it was a bleeding corpse. The generous captor shared the prize with his comrades in the most honourable manner; and shortly after he received a humble message from Colonel Pack, begging a present of the heart, which request was not only complied with, but the kidneys were given in addition.

This was not the only instance of officers being obliged to solicit a meal from privates: just at this very time several of them came and begged a few potatoes from us: those officers who were well liked received a supply with the greatest alacrity on our part, while the tyrannical ones were served with a grudge.

Some of our men having been sent down to a farmhouse for straw, met there with a number of French soldiers on the same errand. Reciprocal civilities passed between them, giving the direct lie to any national antipathy. In the course of the night, we were roused by orders to fall in—no words were to be spoken, or pipes lighted. When we had marched on a short way, one of the men was seized with a violent cramp in the stomach, which set him a roaring like a bull: this noise being contrary to orders, we were forced to answer the poor fellow's cries with blows, to keep him quiet, no other method having any effect.

It was still quite dark, when we marched through the town of Lugo. About this time, several pieces of cannon were buried, and their carriages burned, to prevent the enemy from reaping any benefit by them.

In the middle of the day, we halted in a turnip field. Even that miserable vegetable was considered delicious food; and the whole regiment attacked them as eagerly as famished wolves would have done a dead horse: for my part, never having been able to eat these roots, I was obliged to hush my hunger to sleep; although this, it may be easily conceived, was somewhat difficult. A constant pitiless rain continued to fall.

A party of us having been sent to a farmhouse for straw to litter ourselves in our muddy beds for the night, we received intelligence that apples were discovered up in the loft. This was, indeed, joyful news; hunger lending speed to my heels, I ran with inconceivable velocity to the place; but, alas! every apple had been already bagged, by crowds from every regiment in the army. Bearing up under this misfortune with as much equanimity as possible, I fortunately chanced to enter an unfrequented room in the house, and there discovered a quantity of flour.

Without waiting to feast my eyes long on the glorious sight, I was proceeding to unloose my haversack, when I found myself so benumbed with cold, that I was actually obliged to cut it from my side. Filling our haversacks to the mouth, and taking wisps of straw under our arms, as a kind of excuse, we "went on our way rejoicing," leaving crowds who had scented the precious grain busily engaged in sweeping it into their sacks. Our starving comrades were highly delighted to see us return with such a valuable commodity, instead of worthless straw.

Some hog's-lard being produced, fires were lighted on every side; and some of our most experienced bakers soon made up a quantity of flour cakes, with which we gorged ourselves to our hearts' content. I never tasted a sweeter meal in all my life than this. Although the rain continued with unabated violence, I lay down in the cold mud, and slept as sound as if I had been in the best bed: such are the wonderful effects of a good bellyful after long abstinence: and this proves also, that amidst the most abject misery, there is such a thing as pleasure. Some overplus cakes belonging to me were put into my comrade's haversack, my own being too wet.

We again marched on; but scarcely had I walked an hour, when I lost my shoes, and was obliged to trudge on barefooted. Many of the officers were in the same state; some of them attempted to defend their feet by wrapping pieces of blanket round them. My sufferings were now dreadful; everything in the shape of stockings being long since gone, the constant friction of the wet trousers rubbed the skin completely off my legs, and the raw flesh, feeling as if cauterised, increased my torments to an indescribable degree. But many were in a far worse condition, and lay down completely exhausted with excess of fatigue and misery, waiting impatiently for death to relieve their pangs. The regiments in the immediate rear were, comparatively speaking, in greater distress than ourselves, having, in addition to all our sufferings, the enemy's cavalry to contend with.

Order in the march was now totally disregarded, every regiment in the army being intermixed, on account of the best walkers pressing on, and keeping as near, the van as possible; while the weaker ones either fell behind or fell for ever. Many fell sound asleep while walking, and then stood in the midst of the road like pillars: no attempts were made to awake them, the cry of "Keep off" was raised, and everyone studiously avoided jostling the sleepers. Three successive times did I fall into this strange condition, in spite of myself.

About this time, I saw a dragoon sprawling in the mud, quite drunk, and seemingly unconscious of his miserable situation, laughing and yelling out his *bacchanalian* ribaldry. This poor wretch undoubtedly became food for the crows in a few short hours. Our cavalry and artillery horses died in such numbers, that nearly the whole road between Lugo and Corunna was strewed with their bloated carcasses.

I daily felt more and more the inconvenience of walking with naked feet; and having cut my toe against a stone, I suffered such excruciating pains, that, following the example of others, I threw myself on the ground with a fierce indifference to my fate; death had no longer any terrors for me. While lying in this unenviable condition, I saw General Ferguson, with a number of field-officers and *aides-de-camp*, riding about, entreating all who lay on the ground to get up, as Corunna was near at hand, and, as an additional enticement to get on, the officers cut off a number of knapsacks from the backs of the men.

The general came up to two men who lay close by me, and persuaded them to rise, and crawl on: coming to me next, he attempted to encourage me with hopes of a speedy arrival at the ships, and so on; but I told him in firm, but respectful terms, that "I felt myself unable even to move." I passed a whole night in this condition, bitterly regretting the want of the cakes which had been put in my comrade's haversack. Perhaps some readers may think me a very unsentimental fellow, if I felt only this animal regret at such a time; but they may set their minds at rest when I assure them that home and friends occupied some of my thoughts.

Daylight coming in, the desire of life returned, and a ray of hope darted into my soul; I made a strenuous effort to rise, and succeeded, though I felt as weak as a child. Leaving many on the ground, never to tell the tale again, I staggered on towards a farmhouse which I saw at a distance; and meeting with a pool of water by the way, I walked into it, not with the intention of drowning myself, but of cooling my aching feet, and washing my trowsers. After clawing off a quantity of mud and slime, I arrived at the farmhouse. Here, if I had not been extremely hungry, a whole train of reflections would have burst in upon me, the house being literally *gutted*—not a soul was to be seen. Here was a strong proof of the baneful effects of war; or, in other words, the cruelty of man to man,

Having prowled through every room in the house, without finding anything in the shape of food, I went into the desolate yard, where I spied some beehives in a corner, which, it appears, had escaped the notice of the last plunderers, whoever they were. There being no other means of coming at the honey, I knocked down one of the hives with the but-end of my musquet—for which act it seemed I was likely to pay dear; some of the bees sallied out and stung my feet; perhaps the coldness of the wintry weather prevented the rest from attacking me. I filled my haversack with honey, and after eating as much of it as I could, proceeded on my route.

I soon found that this new sort of food did not agree with me after long abstinence; a sudden sickness came over me, and compelled me to lie down on the road, where I fell asleep. I was awakened from my nap by three of the band who were passing by. One of them, who carried a large loaf, seeing that I had honey; offered to exchange a piece of the loaf for some of it; of course, I eagerly agreed to this, but found, after all, that I could not swallow a morsel of the bread, my weakened jaws refusing to do their duty.

I contrived to hold on my tottering steps for a short distance, and saw by the way four men, of a certain "gallant" Scotch regiment, robbing a poor Spanish woman of some bread, although she was protesting, in the most piteous manner, that she had nothing else to give her starving children. Had not my debilitated state, and the number of my antagonists, prevented me, I would have certainly done everything in my power to prevent such cruelty and injustice: but some little extenuation may be found in the absolute necessity of the case.

I arrived at the town of Batanzas in a very helpless condition. Colonel Pack was looking out of a window when I entered, apparently watching for the arrival of the stragglers of his own regiment: seeing me, he asked what was the number of my company; and on my reply, pointed out the house destined for its reception. I entered with full expectation of being the last that would ever arrive of the whole company, which once consisted of eighty men; but now, to my astonishment, nine only out of that number stood before me. We now had three days' allowance of beef and bread served out; and this was the first expense we had occasioned to our country for a long while.

We were all in such an exhausted state, that even the operation of cooking the provisions was with difficulty accomplished; and this will serve to account for our being highly provoked on discovering, that, during the momentary absence of the cook, who was looking for a knife, the whole of our dinner had been carried off by some heartless villains, thus obliging us to renew our toil in preparing a new mess.

By this time, having got new shoes, some shelter and repose, we started again, somewhat refreshed. We had not gone far, till the sea and Corunna burst on our sight. To describe our feelings at this time would be a waste of words; it is, perhaps, rather musty to compare them to those of the ten thousand Greeks; but, as far as I can judge, the comparison would be a just one. Our joy was, however, a little damped on seeing no ships in readiness; without these we were as badly or rather worse, off than ever. We took up our quarters in a rope-walk on the outskirts of the town of Corunna.

The next morning, we marched out, and encamped by the side of a small rivulet, in order to prevent the enemy from advancing, the stream being fordable at low water. The French had also encamped on the opposite side of the same stream. We lay inactive till next morning, when we were rather alarmed by the blowing up of a powder magazine, about two miles distant: the concussion was so powerful that the ground shook violently under our feet, and the piled arms were levelled with the ground.

On the following day, the 16th of January, 1809, the Battle of Corunna took place; but it so happened that we had little to do with the engagement, only four of our companies being engaged, and those but partially. Towards the close of the day, we were ordered to relieve some of the regiments which had suffered most; in marching across a road to effect this, we saw Sir John Moore carried by wounded. The coming on of night put an end to the action—so that we had to retrace our steps to our old position, having fortunately suffered only the loss of one man killed, an officer and some others wounded.

The history of shooting the cavalry horses is well known; but I confine myself to our own transactions. We bivouacked on the night of the battle, after kindling numerous fires. The ships having arrived, we rose silently in the dead of the night, and leaving some men to keep up the fires, in order to deceive the enemy, we marched off, "*wi little din*," through the town of Corunna, and from thence to the seaside. It was a dark and stormy night; numerous small boats lay pitching and rolling on the troubled waters;'-and our only light came from the *flambeaux* held by some naval officers. The scene of confusion that took place baffles all description; nearly the whole of our army was assembled here, in the most tumultuous manner, and every one rushed indiscriminately into the boats, reckless of danger.

All control and order were now lost, everyone shifting for himself, without regarding the order to keep by his own particular regiment: as usual in such cases, we followed the example, and were soon scattered among the crowd. The confusion was much increased by the turning loose the baggage mules as soon as they were unloaded.

Having, with infinite difficulty, forced my way into a crowded boat, we pulled off from the shore. Already many of the men were asleep at the bottom of the boat—such had been their excessive fatigue. The sailors who rowed us, anxious to get rid of their laborious work, put us on board the vessel nearest to the shore, and the consequence of this was, that the vessels which lay farthest out were not half so much incommoded by numbers as our ship was.

Daylight coming on, the French opened a heavy fire of shot and shells upon the transports, from some batteries on the heights; and this unexpected salute terrified the transport captains so much, that, several of them gave orders to cut their cables, without first taking the necessary precaution to brace their yards. Five vessels, in consequence of this, ran ashore in the greatest disorder. The foolish master of our vessel, seized with the same consternation, (a shell having burst at the stern, filling the whole ship with smoke,) was hastening to follow the rash example the others had set, in cutting the cable, when we thought proper to prevent him.

An officer of the 38th regiment, who seemed to have some nautical skill, then took the command, ordering the sails to be all set first, and afterwards that the cable should be cut. Although the balls were whizzing through the rigging now and then, the officer's orders were obeyed with great promptitude and coolness, and we were soon running out to sea in fine style; not, however, without having the satisfaction of seeing a British seventy-four come in, and silence with a single broadside the battery which had annoyed us so much.

CHAPTER 3

Expedition to Walcheren

Our campaign in the Peninsula had thus ended ingloriously, after a prosperous outset. Such had been exactly the case with the British about a century before. They attempted, under the command of the Earls of Peterborough and Galway, to place Charles the Third on the throne of Spain, in opposition to the wishes of the French and part of the people. Success at first attended them; but the Battle of Almanza compelled them to relinquish all hopes of effecting their design, being obliged to evacuate the country entirely. Till the period of which I speak, this had been the only attempt made by Britain to control Spain, with the exception of some predatory naval attacks. Our own case was, as I have already remarked, similar to that to which I have alluded—it was an attempt to place Ferdinand on the throne in this instance, as in the former, Charles.

It is not difficult to account for our failure; the numerical superiority of Buonaparte's army to that of ours, together with the apathy both of Spaniards and Portuguese to the cause, and other circumstances which I may mention; such as making a winter campaign, by order of our government. If our route be traced on a map, it will be seen, that after leaving Portugal, we passed through the provinces of Estremadura, New Castile, Old Castile, Leon, and Galicia, between the months of October and January; As we advanced northwards from Estremadura, the country became more and more mountainous, till our arrival at Corunna. The year, as it advanced, brought upon us all the horrors of a severe winter. It was never calculated upon, that the climate of the mountainous parts of Spain was so severe.

If, on the contrary, we had remained in the fertile plains of Estremadura, or marched southwards, we should never have felt what we did in this respect, as an eternal spring reigns throughout these districts. A close pursuit for hundreds of miles, without a regular supply of provisions; the ragged state of our clothing; our constant exposure to the damp of the ground; had shoes; and innumerable other inconveniences—all combined, made 6,000 brave fellows bite the dust, or rather the mud. In consequence of this, we were constrained to leave the neighbourhood of this spot, which had been the grave of so many men.

I believe the cause of many deaths, and incalculable sufferings to those who survived their miseries, was owing *solely* to the bad shoes which were furnished to the army by contractors: it was thought a good shoe that would last a week; but the far greater part of them was destroyed in a day or two! Of course, a constant supply could not be kept up at that rate. Many a soldier, poor as he was, would have paid a guinea out of his own pocket cheerfully to get a pair of good shoes,

I must speak here also of the very reprehensible custom of allowing soldiers' wives to follow the army: so far from their being of any service, they were, on the contrary, a constant burden. Washing, which appears naturally a work of theirs, was entirely left to ourselves, not a stitch being ever touched by them. Their profligate lives were not only the detestation of their own husbands, but even of many other soldiers—strange as it may appear in the latter instance.

But to return to my narrative: we were leaving the Iberian shores—"nothing loath;" but we found, to our great inconvenience, that there were 510 of us to be packed on board a very small brig, and the whole of this number had entered the vessel in such disorder, that the amalgamation of our army appeared complete—we having no less than part of seventeen regiments on board. It was found necessary, on account of the crowded state of the ship, to cook at separate times; and, notwithstanding this, it was extremely difficult to find victuals withal; everyone was stealing from another; and serious battles often took place about the privilege of scraping the fragments of burgoo from the sides of the coppers.

It being impossible to stir without trampling on the body of someone or other, the hold continually resounded with the oaths and curses of the individuals trampled on; there was even a man smothered in the course of the voyage, but I believe he was intoxicated at the time. We derived some amusement from an officer who was seldom or never absent from the side of the capstan; during the whole voyage, he was continually rubbing his back against it, having long since given up, as a hopeless case, the idea of freeing himself from the innumerable hordes of vermin by which we were infested. As all of us bore the same torments, but with rather more equanimity than this gentleman, some jokes were played off on him from different quarters.

To our unspeakable joy, we arrived safe at Portsmouth; but cruel fortune seemed not yet tired of castigating us—a sudden gale coming on, compelled us to cut the cable, and allow the vessel to drive on the sands: happily, it abated without doing any serious injury. Some sailors were sent to get us off; this, however, it required several tides to effect. These rude sons of Neptune were always coming and going to and from the vessel, and as they often looked down the hold, they cracked many jokes upon our evident misery.

All the men belonging to the other regiments having been taken ashore left us abundant room. We were soon floated into deep water, and the rest of the regiment now joined us; but still we were all detained on board—I never could learn for what reason, the rest of the army having been already landed.

Among the women who were put ashore on our arrival at Portsmouth, there was one belonging to our regiment who had rather the appearance of a bundle of rags than of a human being. Upon some of the men calling out to her not to expose the regiment, by telling the good English people that such a scarecrow belonged to it, she answered, that she would soon have more prize-money than any of us. This eventually turned out truth; not long afterwards she joined us again, finely dressed, and having 30*l*. in her pocket: she had procured all this by begging:—her lamentable story had taken well; but, I dare say, she got the money more readily on account of having a beautiful child in her arms.

Being all transferred to a different vessel, we were ordered round to Ramsgate, in order to disembark. In passing Beachyhead we got a sudden alarm, by the vessel heeling so much that her yards were in the water. A sergeant and twelve men were thrown from their births to the bottom of the hold; the guns, coppers, and other moveable articles broke loose; and a general cry was raised that we were going down. The danger did not prevent some would- be-wits from saying, that there was a "sergeant's command away to the hold." In the course of this short voyage, I got my only shirt stolen off the rigging while it was drying; but my rage was soothed by new shirts and trowsers being served out to every man of us.

Having landed at Ramsgate, we marched to Ashford barracks. Here the old tyrant Death again visited us, and the 91st regiment in particular, with a heavy hand—three or four men dying every day for some time, in consequence of brain fever: this was universally allowed to arise from their former fatigues.

We now marched to Braeburnlees, and received a draft of 350 recruits from Scotland, besides a number of men volunteered into our corps from some English and Irish militia regiments. These reinforcements made us 1,100 strong, and we formed as beautiful a regiment as I ever saw; very different in appearance from what we were on our arrival from Spain. In June 1809 we marched to Portsmouth, and encamped there, while the rest of the army was assembling for the invasion of Walcheren.

The fatal expedition to Walcheren had now been determined upon. We accordingly embarked in the *Belleisle*, 74-gun ship, having, in addition to our men, some horses and artillery on board. Having proceeded to Deal, we sailed from that place at three o'clock in the morning, on the 28th of July, 1809. Never will I forget the glorious sight of the most powerful and numerous fleet which ever left the British shores—the sea looked as if it groaned under the weight of so many vessels, and as far as the eye could reach a wilderness of masts was seen. Thirty-five sail of the line, twenty-three frigates, 179 transports, and an innumerable quantity of small craft, composed this mighty armament, containing 39,000 troops, under the command of the Earl of Chatham.

What wonderful revolutions does time make! scarcely nineteen centuries ago, Caesar invaded Britain with a numerous fleet, and found the inhabitants immersed in the grossest barbarism, and utterly ignorant of sea affairs. Little did he think, I date say, that the descendants of these very islanders would send forth ships to subdue countries in every quarter of the globe, and reign everywhere undisputed masters of the sea; still less did he think, that one of their smallest frigates would have been sufficient to put the whole of his 800 sail to flight.

But to return from this digression:—thirteen hours' sailing enabled us to drop our anchors off the island of Walcheren, at four o'clock in the afternoon. Next day, the whole army got into the boats, which all started at a signal for the shore; the landing was successfully performed, one battery only having attempted to annoy us, and that without effect. Seeing some of the enemy lurking in a wood, two of our companies rushed forward, took two pieces of cannon, and some prisoners.

We marched towards Campveer; some of our men entered a fort by the way, which the enemy had evacuated on our approach, and found a good dinner, which the French had left, ready cooked. It was quite dark when we arrived at the town of Campveer; but though we trod as lightly as possible, the French sentinel discovered and challenged us. Immediately after this, a tremendous fire of grape-shot was opened upon us; but as the garrison fired merely at random, on account of the darkness, we did not suffer so much as if it had been otherwise.

However, the scene was appalling enough—there was a constant roar of the guns, the bullets were whizzing audibly, and were crushing or lopping off the branches of the surrounding trees. While in this situation, I was suddenly struck to the ground by a ball which had entered the side of my knapsack; fortunately, I escaped unhurt. Finding that we were exposing ourselves needlessly to danger, we retreated, with a loss of sixty killed and wounded;—a heavy price indeed, since there had been nothing accomplished. We were obliged to lie all night on the bank of a muddy ditch, with the rain lashing on us the whole time. Being very thirsty, after our midnight wanderings, we were fain to content ourselves with drinking the disgusting and putrid ditch-water.

On examining my knapsack, I found the ball had gone through a pair of shoes, broken a soap-box and button-stick to pieces, and finally lodged in a shirt, after passing through eleven folds of it. I kept this ball for some time, but at last threw it away, it being a quarter of a pound in weight, and too heavy to carry.

Next day we marched round the town—I presume the intention was to discover its most assailable point. Several shot and shells were thrown at us in doing this, but without doing us any damage. Our guns were hauled by a number of sailors from the fleet; these fellows being utterly ignorant of land operations, were continually using their sea terms in dragging; such as starboard, and larboard, and so forth.

We had some difficulty in keeping them to their work; on one occasion, the whole body disappeared, nobody knew whither, till some Dutchmen came up and informed us, with great agitation, that the tars had forced their way into the houses, and were making some rude attacks on the *frows*. Upon receiving this intelligence, we went forward, and drove them back to the guns at the point of the bayonet.

Finding that nothing could be done in the way of entering the strong town of Campveer, we continued our march to a small village in its environs, and saw on the way a French frigate on fire. She had been endeavouring to escape up the Scheldt, but having grounded in the attempt, the crew had set fire to her: as usual, every gun went off as the flames came to it.

We encamped that night in a hay-field, and a party of us

was sent for water; however, not a drop was to he had, except that of the ditches; this miserable island being totally destitute of springs. One of the men seeing a jar in an empty boat, stept on board with the idea of its containing gin—he raised it to his head, and actually swallowed some of the liquid before he discovered that it was rank train oil. We got plenty of cheap gin in the village; there was as much given for a sixpence as for a shilling—the honest Hollanders not seeming to have the smallest idea of the respective value of English money.

Some sharpers among us, seeing the poor people's ignorance in this respect, furbished up their own copper coins, and covering them with quicksilver, passed them off for English coin with great ease; nay, sometimes by merely knocking the eye off a button, and flattening it, the workman obtained the value of a shilling. I cannot help laughing, to think of an old woman, who kept a kind of grocery shop, giving copper coins to our men in change, and in a few hours afterwards taking them back as sixpences!

Leaving our encampment, we marched on, passing through the town of Middleburg in the night-time; and still continuing our march, we came unawares, in the dusk of the morning, under the guns of fort Ramekins; our first warning was given by the enemy's fire, but we made a precipitate retreat, without suffering loss. Having arrived within a short distance of Flushing, we lay there till the rest of the army came up.

Vigorous preparations were now made to bombard the town of Flushing, and our constant employment was, for some time, building a battery. The French, as a last resource, cut the sea dike, with the hope of cramping the operations of the British forces: this was obviated, however, by placing sticks at intervals along the edges of the paths, in the vicinity of Flushing; this precaution enabled us to guide our steps with safety when the full tide inundated the island. A battery, which the enemy had raised near ours, annoyed us exceedingly; we could not march out to relieve our picquet, without a fire being opened upon the men.

It was therefore resolved upon to attempt the surprisal of this grievous plague. One dark night, two parties were formed; one of them was ordered to advance silently, and storm the battery; the other to follow in the rear, and fill up the cut in the dike if necessary. Everything succeeded as well as could be wished; the first party met with no obstruction till they stumbled over a French drummer: this poor fellow was preparing to beat an alarm, when that trouble was saved him by his being thrown over into the sea, drum and all. Nothing powerful enough presented itself to stop the party's progress; they pressed on, bore down all opposition, took the battery, spiked the guns, secured some prisoners, and returned with a loss of thirty-eight killed and wounded.

Meanwhile our sanguinary bombarding was going on both from land and sea; the ear was stunned with the continual roar of the artillery and the hissing of the rockets; and the heart bled at the sufferings of the devoted Flushing people. Night, the usual time of suspending hostilities, gave no respite: the darkness was dispelled by the burning of the houses, set on fire by the shells; of these articles I have counted fourteen in the air at one time—such was the immense number thrown. By day the line-of-battle ships ranged close to the town, and poured in their tremendous broadsides, then, wheeling round, the dose was repeated from the other sides; I could discern distinctly the dreadful effects of each broadside, an immense cloud of dust marking the place, where perhaps a stately building stood the moment before!

The resistance offered to us was, comparatively speaking, feeble; and it appeared afterwards, that the wily Frenchmen had compelled the unfortunate citizens to work the guns against us, and, by keeping aloof, saved their own bacon; the chief loss thus fell upon the Hollanders, both in lives and effects. Four days of incessant battering having reduced Flushing to a heap of smoking ruins, the French finding that their situation was no longer tenable, surrendered at discretion. Having seen the garrison march out prisoners of war, we proceeded to Middleburgh.

About this time, that fatal sickness which conducted so many to their last home, made its appearance: the medical men were as yet unaware of what the complaint was, or what it arose from; they knew not that it was the ague, that scourge of marshy countries. Continuing our march, we arrived once more at Campveer, the place being now in our possession. Here we found the troops in a deplorable state; disease and death were reigning triumphant. The 84th regiment, which we were appointed to relieve, was already seized with the disease—the men were nearly all sick or dead; the 68th and 85th were in the same predicament shortly afterwards, their shattered remains were therefore sent off to England, by which means we were left alone in the town.

It was soon found that we were not to pass the ordeal of Campveer ague with impunity, as a very short time sufficed to throw upwards of 700 men into the hospitals, and return 200 in a sort of convalescent state. I was among the latter number, that is to say, neither absolutely sick nor in health, and subject at times to fits of ague: sometimes a dozen men were to be seen shivering with this complaint at the same time in the barrack-room. As a preventive to the increase of the disease, we were often drawn up, and jugs of bark served out from rear to front.

Three hundred of the guards, who were sent over from South Beveland to our hospital, in a sickly state, died off nearly to a man; this constrained us to be continually engaged in the disgusting employment of burying them, as well as the dead of our own corps. A whole field had been completely filled with bodies, when the excessive fatigue of this occupation, united to our weakened constitutions, made it necessary afterwards for us to employ the inhabitants in the doleful service.

Little else but a succession of the same horrors occurred during our stay of three months in this den of pestilence. We remarked that the town's people had carefully picked up the shells and rockets, which we had formerly thrown into the place while in possession of the French, and built them into the very apertures they had made in the walls of the houses: I presume the citizens intended that the warlike missives should thus stand conspicuously, as so many mementos to future generations, to show their forefathers' sufferings. I remember a story of some of our sailors, who belonged to one of the numerous guard boats which patrolled the coast, landing on the island of Beveland, and surprising a French picket, consisting of three men and a corporal.

The sailors, not content with making them prisoners, burnt their guardhouse; and saying that it was a damned pity to take away the fellows without their house, the big children actually heaved a heavy sentry-box upon their shoulders, and brought it in along with the prisoners, groaning and sweating under the preposterous load.

Only a few days before our final evacuation of the island, I was attacked in a serious manner with the Walcheren sickness. To describe the torments of the ague cannot be interesting; however, I may state some of the sensations I felt: first, a sort of listlessness pervades the mind, accompanied with frequent yawning, the feet get cold, the cold then gradually ascends to the back, and in fact through the whole body; a universal icy shivering, and a chattering of the teeth, next ensue, followed by an ardent thirst; during the whole progress of the disorder the nails of the fingers are perfectly white.

Two days before the regiment took its departure I was sent off to Flushing; embarking from thence in a small boat, to go out to the transport, I was attacked by severe fits of the ague, in consequence of the waves dashing over the vessel and wetting me to the skin: I was obliged to be hauled up the side of the transport nearly at the last gasp. After riding at anchor till the rest of the fleet was ready, we set sail for England, seeing first the docks and storehouses of Flushing set on flames, to prevent the enemy from reaping any advantage from them. While we were upwards of three miles from the Flanders shore, a 24lb. ball came from a fort there, shattered our windlass, and, continuing its course, struck off a sergeant's legs in the headquarter-ship!

On our arrival off Deal, I was placed along with a number of other invalids, in a boat, to be towed ashore by another boat manned with sailors: before we had gone far, it was discovered that the plug was out, and that the water was rushing in upon us;—it had risen already to our knees, when the sailor who steered jumped suddenly into the other boat among his comrades, under the pretext of getting us better towed; we soon perceived, however, that the heartless wretches were making preparations to cast off the towing line, and abandon us to our fate.

The water was by this time up to the gunwale—the deep was yawning for its prey, and we felt by anticipation our dying struggles—when we were suddenly relieved from our despondency, by one of our men starting up, loading his piece, and pointing it into the other boat:—this kind of argument was irresistible to the "*gallant British tars*;" they instantly laid aside their villainous intentions, and the steersman came back with a very downcast look.

A foraging cap was now stuffed into the leak, the plug was shortly after found, the towing was resumed, hope began to "tell a flattering tale," till the beach was reached, when it was found that no small dexterity was required to land us, on account of a heavy surf beating on the shore. A party of soldiers belonging to a Welsh regiment was employed here to carry us ashore; this was performed by wading up to their middles, and lifting us on their backs; in this manner the whole party was landed safely, except four men, to wit, myself, two German soldiers, and another man—the boat having been unexpectedly driven on its side by a chance wave: it soon righted, however, but not without putting us in imminent jeopardy of our lives by drowning.

We were at length dragged ashore, like drowned rats, and placed in a waggon, to be carried to Deal. Just at that very moment, the inspiring notes of some well-known bugles burst on my ear; I could not be mistaken, the 71st had landed about the same time as myself—how much did I regret that there was no opportunity of joining them! But my debilitated state effectually prevented that.

I was now in the Deal hospital, where the greatest attention was paid me, particularly by an orderly man of the hospital, whom I discovered to be a native of Glasgow. He took me to his own ward, and administered to my wants with the utmost kindness and solicitude, during the whole time that I was in the place, which was three weeks. Such is the strange nature of mankind, that, merely because I drew my breath first among a certain heap of stones, another man, coming from the same heap, should do everything in his power to serve me; whereas, had I unfortunately belonged to any other place, perhaps it would have stood hard with me, if I ever recovered.

It would, perhaps, be considered improper in me to dwell long in making remarks upon the hackneyed subjects of the folly of ministers in ordering such an invasion as that of Walcheren; the imbecility of the commander of the land forces; and the inexpediency of bombarding Flushing. That the expedition was miserably disastrous, both in the loss of lives among the soldiers, and in the waste of money to the nation, no one can deny; but it is doing no more than justice to the planners of it, to say, that they had not the remotest idea of the banefulness of the climate, although so near it—a fact unexampled in history; and this, as it is well known, was the primary cause of our ill success. As to the general, I believe he did everything in his power to fulfil his orders; with the exception, perhaps, of being rather dilatory. The bombardment of Flushing was, in my humble opinion, preferable to the dreadful effects of storming the place.

It is also superfluous to descant upon the manners, and customs of the Dutch; the contiguousness of their country to England would form of itself a palpable reason for this. For instance, their universal habit of cleanliness, and their practice of smoking tobacco, are well known even to the most illiterate people,

I now joined the regiment at Braeburnlees; but finding myself still unwell, I obtained leave of absence for three months, and went home to Glasgow. The ague continued to stick close by me nearly the whole time I was there. An old sailor advised me to take some brandy mixed with gunpowder; it might be imagination, but after swallowing this rough medicine, I found myself gradually getting better.

Leaving old Glasgow once more, I returned to the south. Coming up in the London smack, two hours after leaving Leith, one of the passengers entered into a conversation with me, inquiring if I had been at Walcheren, the number of my regiment, whether I would like best to be a sailor or a soldier, and such like chit-chat: the steward at this time calling the cabin passengers to tea, the stranger went down along with them, but soon came up again, carrying a porringer of tea and a roll—these he politely forced me to accept. Next day, another passenger, who had the appearance of an English traveller, tired, seemingly, with the monotony of a sea life, challenged, for a pastime, any of the company to ascend to the mast-head with him; none but the stranger took him up.

They both accordingly climbed to the very top; but, in conformity to the usual custom, two sailors mounted after them, and tied the traveller to the mast, where he hung, the laughing-stock of every passenger, until he promised to pay a bottle of rum to the crew. The traveller now came down, I dare say rather nettled at the issue of his exploit, and at the stranger for not being tied up also. I was not near enough to distinguish every word, but I could plainly discover that high words were likely to ensue between the climbers; this, however, was suddenly put a stop to, by the steward whispering into the traveller's ear, that he was speaking to Lord Cochrane.

The Englishman was dumb instantly:—such is the effect of a title, a great name, or the possession of money, that even the most independent-spirited man is involuntarily awed for a time by such advantages, although he may be in the right. It was through these means that I found out that my generous and truly noble entertainer, and Lord Cochrane, were one and the same person.

Having again joined the regiment at Braeburnlees, we marched off to Deal, where we lay till the month of September; 600 of the most effective men in the regiment were then picked out to serve in the Peninsula: the rest of the corps had not yet recovered from the effects of their Walcheren trip. I was thought efficient enough to be enrolled among the former number: our commander was by this time changed. Colonel Pack having gone into the Portuguese service: the command was now jointly swayed by the Colonels Peacock and Reynolds.

CHAPTER 4

French Retreat, Our Advance

Two frigates having been appointed to take us out, we embarked at Deal, and sailed next morning. This voyage was as prosperous as could be expected—fourteen days' sailing enabling, us to land at Black-horse Square, Lisbon, on the 28th of September, 1810. We lay some days in the city; camp equipage was then served out, the soldiers' wives who had children were all obliged to remain—express orders being given to that effect. Having been thus freed from all unnecessary impediments, we marched up the country to join that army which had been reaping its laurels at Talavera, about the very time we were sailing to fill the fenny graves of Walcheren.

Arriving at Mafra, a palace belonging to the King of Portugal, we were quartered in it for a few days. The sergeants, who were sent before us to allot the different lodgings to the men, found the upper apartments swarming with such hosts of fleas, that when we entered the place, we beheld the sergeants stripped naked, banging their clothes against the walls, in order to shake out these petty but troublesome enemies. It was then found absolutely necessary for us to evacuate the best places in the house, and retire to the ground flat, where there was a stone floor—resigning thus, for comfort's sake, every idea of contending longer with the fleas; no doubt a wonderful triumph to the insect world over armed men.

About this time Colonel Cadogan joined us, having been appointed to the command of the regiment. He made an animating speech to us on this occasion, the substance of which was—his satisfaction at obtaining the command of our "heroic corps,"—a command which he had long ardently panted for—his hopes of having the honour to lead us on to higher achievements than we had ever yet performed, and so on.

Continuing our march, we fell in with immense numbers of the unfortunate Portuguese people, who had been literally turned out of house and hall; they were travelling towards Lisbon, as the only place of refuge from the baleful influence of the contending armies. A large tract of country had been laid waste, and their houses desolated, to prevent the French from receiving supplies in the pursuit of our army, which it seems was retreating with rapid strides towards the coast. The wretched and emaciated looks of the Portuguese travellers were truly piteous to a feeling heart; some of them were mounted on cars, such as sick and children; but by far the greater number were crawling painfully along on their feet: I particularly remarked many frail old women endeavouring to support their tottering steps with staffs.

The sufferings of many a British inhabitant have been, and are at times, great; but the above-mentioned sight convinced me, that we have endured but little in comparison to the Portuguese. Unless we go back as far as the times of Cromwell, the Pretender, or prior to those unhappy periods—our country has remained for a long time in happy ignorance of the real horrors of war.

We now saw Lord Wellington for the first time since the Battle of Vimiera; and soon after we arrived at the town of Sobral. Here we met our army in full retreat from the field of Busaco; this battle had been fought only two days before we landed in Portugal. A woeful change had taken place in the appearance of Sobral since I saw it last; then a more beautiful or lively place never existed; but now the houses were gutted, the gardens destroyed, and the busy hum of its former inhabitants hushed: a half-starved hog or two might occasionally be seen stealing along the deserted streets; but these, with an old crippled woman, who could not make her escape, and a cat, were the only natives of the place to be found. However, as part of the army (our own regiment was in the number) took up quarters for the night in the town, the solemn stillness was soon dissolved: military bustle is well calculated to banish all romantic reflections.

Towards the close of next day, the enemy made their appearance: we were purposely left alone to engage them, being supposed to be fresher than the rest of the army, who were much knocked up by their laborious retreat: perhaps it might also have been intended that we should come in for a share of the fighting, and make up our lee-way in that respect. Notwithstanding our best efforts to the contrary, the Frenchmen drove us out of the town, though not without a good deal of difficulty; they at length retreated in their turn. We bivouacked that night midway between the French and British Armies, but marched back in the morning, and occupied Sobral again.

Half of our company was now sent out on picket; I remained along with the other half, in a house where a quantity of dried fish was found; this, in addition to plenty of rice and Indian corn, contributed materially to making us all very merry; for the immediate prospect of meat draws forth cheerfulness at once from hungry men. An oven being in the place, many set to and baked abundance of bread, not only with the intention of filling their bellies, but their haversacks besides; our "here today and gone tomorrow" sort of life, putting us under the necessity of breaking the Christian mandate of "take no heed for tomorrow."

But, alas! we were unexpectedly roused from these *intellectual* enjoyments, by orders to turn out, and join the picket on the outside of the town. Catching up our firelocks with some reluctance, we issued forth, and effected the junction. Scarcely had we done so, when General Erskine rode up, and ordered us to retreat, as the enemy were advancing. By the time we had retraced our steps back to the town, we found the rest of the regiment drawn up under arms: the general then ordered two companies to post themselves on a neighbouring hill, which was thickly covered with vines.

The intention of this was, to amuse the enemy, as it were, while we were effecting our escape. The French, both infantry and cavalry, were by this time nearly close to us; they presented a numerous and imposing front—we were, therefore, again obliged to suffer ourselves to be driven through the town at double quick time: hurrying past the house we had left with so much regret, one of us ran in at a venture, and brought out a loaf from the oven, at the expense of a burnt hand.

At length we halted from our race at the outside of the town; the two companies soon after made their appearance, closely pursued by the French. The vine trees which they had to force through in their flight had the usual peculiarity of catching a tenacious hold of any person who presumes to invade their territories, especially if he is in haste; this being the case with our comrades, it was with some difficulty that they surmounted the obstacles which both the French and the vines threw in their way. They now joined us, having, upon the whole, covered our retreat with great skill, and succeeded in attracting much of the enemy's attention.

Just as they came up to us, one of them received a ball from the French, in some part or other of his body, the sudden smart of which made him spring up several feet in the air, in the same manner that a cock does: we were inconsiderate enough to raise a horse laugh at the man's misfortune, but this was rather at the oddity of his behaviour in receiving it.

The enemy having for the present ceased hostilities, we bivouacked for the night in a ploughed field; no comfortable bed, indeed, considering that we had, in addition, a high wind and frequent showers of rain. Next day, having got on our greatcoats and bonnet covers, the enemy attacked us with greater vigour and resolution than ever. We heard afterwards that this extraordinary fierceness was occasioned by their taking us for Portuguese, on account of our change of dress: it is necessary to say here, that the French had hitherto been accustomed to drive the Portuguese like sheep before them. A continual skirmishing was kept up the whole day, from behind walls and other places of ambush.

At one time, the enemy came on in such overwhelming

numbers, that we were obliged to retreat rather precipitately over a wall. One of our men, named Rae, a native of Paisley, and the oldest man in the regiment; not being so active in ascending the wall as the rest of us, and perhaps being apprehensive of receiving a bayonet thrust *par derrière* while doing so, he chose courageously to stand his ground alone: the first enemy that approached he shot dead, the next he bayoneted, a third shared the same fate—and the ancient hero then coolly effected his retreat.

Another man, while coming over the wall, received no less than a dozen of bullets through his greatcoat and canteen, without suffering a single wound in any part of his body. But another poor fellow did not escape so well; he had, for security's sake, cunningly pulled as many stones out of the wall as would admit the barrel, of his musquet. While he was in a crouching attitude, preparing to keep up an incessant fire on the enemy from his loophole, a ball came from them, and, by a remarkable accident, entered the very aperture and his eye at the same instant, leaving him dead on the spot.

Before the heat of the engagement came on, we were honoured with a visit from an officer who had held, not long before, a high rank in the regiment. We were rather surprised at his unusual boldness, in coming without compulsion to a place where there was danger, as it had hitherto been notorious to us all, that when there was anything like fighting in the case, the gentleman in question would rather have been in Lapland.

But our wavering doubts of his returning courage were soon dissipated, in consequence of two or three balls from the French whistling through the air: this unexpected salute so petrified the unhappy hero, that he cried to us in a palpitating voice, "He was afraid *his horse* would be shot." Looking round then, and dreading the approach of more leaden almonds, he told us to tell Colonel Cadogan that "he had called upon him;" so saying, he galloped off like lightning, amidst the sneers of the soldiery. Perhaps, after all, such a man as this deserves pity rather than contempt.

General Erskine and Colonel Cadogan having been eye-witnesses of Rae's bravery, afterwards ordered him to be presented with a medal, bearing the following inscription:

To John Rae,
for his exemplary courage and good
conduct as a Soldier, at Sobral,
14th October, 1810.

He also had the offer of being appointed to the rank of a sergeant, but this he refused: he was a man of a gloomy disposition; in short, a Methodist. It is remarkable enough, that the medal was made out of a common dollar, by one of the men, in a manner which would have done no discredit to the best silversmith: this man had never been bred to such a profession, but was of an ingenious turn in all respects.

The din of war having ended, we now got time to look around us. It was found, in the first place, that the ploughed field we stood upon had got so wet with the heavy rain, that it was with difficulty anyone could walk over it; no sooner was one foot dragged forward, than the other sunk deep, and stuck fast in the soil: in fact, our appearance could, without exaggeration, have been compared to that of bees among tar. One man, who, I presume, had been a weaver, tormented by the pains of his former fatigue, and the annoyance of his present state, was heard to exclaim, that he would rather be working an *"eight and twa"* at home than be at this work.

When the sun had sunk beneath the horizon, or, in other words, when it was dark, we retreated over a hill where a fort was situated; its proper name I know not, but among us it went by the name of the Black Battery: this was the utmost point which the enemy advanced to, in the direction of Lisbon, at this time. We now arrived at a village, where we took up our quarters. We were joined at this place by the 50th and 92nd regiments, which had just landed in Portugal. Continuing our progress, we arrived and halted at Sobreira: the enemy had by this time occupied Sobral, which being only a mile distant from us, consequently the enemy's sentinels and our own were quite close to each other. Constant employment was now given us as labourers. We were engaged in cutting down, for instance, many orange groves, to build breast-works, or, properly speaking, assisting in the formation of those famous lines which baffled the skill and utmost efforts of Massena to penetrate.

The lines being completely finished, we lay in sight of the enemy for six weeks. Few important events took place all that while.

Having little to do, we sometimes employed ourselves in searching for the corn which the Portuguese had hid under ground; our system of doing this was, to find out a particular. place where the ground sounded hollow at the stamp of a foot. When such a discovery was made, a ramrod was driven down to prove the presence of the grain: by these means great quantities were often found. A house which lay between the enemy's picket and our own, was greatly famed for containing a good store of wine, which of course had no owner, or at least nobody knew or cared where he was: the news of this drew the bibbers of both armies in flocks to the place.

Many were to be seen slipping cautiously out, to evade the observation of the sentinels, and repairing to the general rendezvous: a form of politeness was kept up even there—the British waiting on the outside of the house till the French soldiers had satisfied themselves with the "rosy wine;" they then went in to the same work, while the French waited in their turn to renew the attack. Before the road to this house had been universally known, some of our men met a Highlander returning from it, half-seas-over: they asked him several questions, such as, if the liquor was good; but the only reply that could be drawn from Donald was, "*that it is sin but sousands o't,*" meaning thereby, that the wine was thin, but plenty of it.

One day, some of the men being out in search of oranges, a young Irish lad, one of the party, fell by some means or other into the hands of the French. Sometime after this, in the course of the enemy's retreat, we found him extended on the road, so reduced by hunger, sickness, and fatigue, that nobody knew him, not even his own brother, who was also in the regiment: the poor wretch was at last only recognised by some marks on his clothes: he died, however, soon afterwards.

Another day I saw Marshal Massena come down pretty near us, accompanied only by two or three of his staff: he was apparently reconnoitring our position, taking several peeps through a telescope in our direction. Although the marshal was completely within our reach, no one thought of firing at him, as we knew that the French would be as honourable as ourselves in this respect, if they had the same opportunity. At the end of six weeks, as I said before, the enemy relinquished their blockade, and decamped in the night-time, without beat of drum, in consequence of their provisions being entirely exhausted. It was the middle of the following day before we discovered their retreat; the lines were in consequence evacuated with great speed, and an immediate pursuit commenced.

While we were passing hurriedly through the town of Sobral once more, some legible chalked letters on a door met our eyes—they were to this effect, "*two of the 71st here*:" some of us went accordingly into the house, and found two of our men, who had been taken prisoners by the French; both of the unfortunate fellows were disabled, by the loss of a leg each. The humane attention of the enemy, in guiding us to their assistance, deserves some applause: I question if the warriors of any other nation but the French and British would have had the generosity to perform such an action.

In the course of the pursuit, a party of our cavalry having captured some French prisoners, and brought them in, to deliver them to the charge of Colonel Cadogan—a sergeant was sent along with them, to point out the way to his quarters. While the sergeant was doing this, walking at the head of the cavalcade, he fell accidentally into a draw-well. This occurrence alarmed the prisoners, who supposed that the sudden vanishing of the unfortunate guide was a trick to decoy them to an untimely end: however, he was hauled out, after having stood for some time up to the chin in water.

After continuing the pursuit for some days, our headquarters were established at Cartaxo, the enemy having halted at Santarem, with the resolution of standing their ground. We then marched to the vicinity of the latter place, in expectation of giving battle; but it was soon discovered that the French had posted themselves in such an advantageous position, that any effort of ours to dislodge them would be ineffectual. We lay before the town a whole day, during which time Colonel Cadogan, with the intention of creating amusement, set every trade in the regiment to run races with each other; the victors were rewarded with rum: the tailors and shoemakers, I recollect, had a keen contest.

In the evening we marched to a village, to take up quarters: through some mistake, a party of us and; a party of the 92nd were told off, or billeted, on the same house. Fortunately for us, we had taken possession of it first, as it was not long till the 92nd party appeared, demanding admittance, and commanding us, in an imperious tone, to turn out: this hard condition was absolutely refused, it being a very wet rough night; upon which they sent for their colonel, thinking, no doubt, to terrify us into submission by this means: but on his arrival, our officer answered his blustering threats by sternly repeating our fixed determination to remain where we were.

Finding that it was impossible to effect an entrance, they quietly retreated, to roost in some other place; where, I know not. Our excitation had been so great, that I verily believe blood would have been shed ere our expulsion could have been effected. Next day we marched to Almastairs, and were quartered there in a nunnery and a convent contiguous to one another.

Truly, little respect was paid here to the sanctity of the Catholic religion by the men; many of them were to be seen washing their shirts in the holy water fonts; one fellow also took the wooden image of a saint, and threw it into a fire which was kindled at the chapel door, crying at the same time, "Down with popery!" A Highland officer belonging to the 92nd happened unluckily to enter at the time, and seeing this, was so shocked and scandalised at the supposed sacrilege of the action (being a

Catholic himself), that he expressed himself to this effect: "*You seventy-furst will cum to a pad end one tay.*"

The French had only evacuated the nunnery the night before our arrival; they had, with the mischievous taste of monkeys, torn and destroyed a number of books and papers belonging to the nuns, and, in short, turned everything topsy-turvy: it must be owned, however, that we were not backward in completing the work of destruction, as all the movable furniture was broken down and used up for our firewood.

All thoughts of disturbing the enemy at Santarem being given up for the present, we moved on to the deserted village of Alcintrina, and there took up our winter quarters. The weather being cold, and having nothing to shelter ourselves but the naked walls of the houses, we were put to great shifts for the sake of snugness at night: we had then to take off part of our clothes, to serve as a kind of couches, counterpanes were formed by greatcoats, and our legs being thrust through the sleeves gave additional warmth. Our time in this place was passed rather monotonously; however, every kind of amusement that we could invent was put in practice.

The officers often exercised themselves by riding horse and ass races; games of football and cricket were also instituted; besides occasional dances, to the sound of the bagpipe. At other times, we had recourse to our old plan of proving the ground with ramrods: corn and clothes were generally the fruits of our labour; but at one time something like a box was felt: fired with the hope of gold, or some other rich prize, all around fell to digging up the earth; but, alas! when the object of our search was exposed to view, it proved to be a coffin, containing the body of a Portuguese.

The place being at some distance from any burying-ground, we were the more surprised at the discovery; in fact, it is the universal custom of that country to bury the dead under churches. However, without questioning whether the knife of the assassin, or the excommunication of the priest, had caused the corpse to be placed here, we closed the coffin, and put it into its former situation, leaving the ashes to moulder, unseen more by mortal eye.

At length, about the beginning of March 1811, the enemy retreated from their strong position at Santarem: in consequence of this, we broke up our quarters, and joined in the pursuit, passing by the way through the village of Torres Novas. Every day the advanced guard of our army and the enemy's rearguard were engaged. The miserable effects of a rapid retreat began already to be visible; we were continually passing over the bodies of men and horses who had been slain, wounded, or knocked up by fatigue; but not one of the human beings was alive, in consequence of the crowds of cowardly Portuguese ruffians, who were hanging constantly on the way, killing and stripping every man that lay helpless on the ground.

This was all done, under the specious pretence of patriotism, and the desire of avenging the injuries they had received from the French: but the true nature of these jackals was soon discovered, and the direct lie given to their patriotic professions, by their murdering indiscriminately every Briton, as well as Frenchman, who was so unfortunate as to be unable to offer resistance; besides, all of them carried large sacks to contain the spoils of the victims. We got so exasperated at the conduct of these fellows, that they, for security's sake, always carried on their unhallowed work at a respectful distance from us.

However, it must be owned, that the French retaliated in the most cruel manner; and, it is more than probable, the innocent, not the guilty, were the chief sufferers. Every house and village we came to was found in flames, and the fate of their inhabitants was horrible to the last degree. Scott, in his *Vision* of Don Roderick, describes their miseries thus:—

> O, triumph for the fiends of lust and wrath!
> Ne'er to be told, yet ne'er to be forgot,
> What wanton horrors mark'd their wrackful path!
> The peasant butchered in his ruined cot,
> The hoary priest even at the altar shot.
> Childhood and age given o'er to sword and flame,

Woman to infamy;—no crime forgot.
By which inventive demons might proclaim
Immortal hate to man, and scorn of God's great name!
The rudest sentinel, in Britain bora,
With horror paused to view the havoc done,
Gave his poor crust to feed some wretch forlorn,
Wiped his stern eye, then fiercer grasped his gun.

Such was the extremity of hunger among the Portuguese, that it was common to see them eagerly picking up and eating the grains of corn at the places where cavalry horses were fed. Having arrived at the town of Pombal, where a part of the army was engaged, we continued advancing. The awful spectacle of the whole town of Condacia in flames next engaged our attention: this place appears to have been a fashionable resort of the Portuguese nobility and gentry, the houses being all stately and magnificent; but a sad change was rapidly taking place—a devouring fire raging unchecked on both sides of the streets as we marched through.

I have no wish to extenuate the excesses of the French Army in this retreat;—on the contrary, I think I felt just as much for the Portuguese as the common run of people did; yet there are some circumstances which ought to be recollected. Had the British been placed in the same predicament as the French were,—that is to say, had they been the enemies and invaders of Portugal, they would have found it to be a very different thing from being friendly allies; they would have found that they had to contend with a treacherous and ferocious set of people, who neglected no means, however base or unworthy, to cut off an inoffensive straggling soldier; besides having, in addition, to cope with an army of foreigners as valiant as themselves.

These grievances would have, in consequence, roused and goaded them on to revenge; the nature of war also having a tendency to render the heart callous and to brutify the mind, they would, excited by blind fury, have been induced to go farther in their retaliation than the rules of justice prescribed: in short, I have little hesitation in saying, that the British would have committed the same enormities as the French did, had they been in the same situation.

Another thing is, the French Army was far from being composed wholly of Frenchmen;—the unceasing wars of Buonaparte had drained France of men, the deficiencies were therefore made up out of conquered countries, such, as Germany and Italy—consequently the natives of these countries were mercenaries, having no cause to fight for: as whatever victory they might contribute to gain, they knew that the French alone would have all the credit, they therefore determined that their masters should have all the odium too,—so that there is little doubt, but that the mercenaries were thus the principal perpetrators of the before-mentioned cruelties.

Away then with our vulgar prejudices against the French: let us look at our proceedings in India, or in the American war, where Germans were also employed; having done so, it is highly hypocritical to exclaim against the French in the present case, or to say more than deplore in general the deteriorating effects of war.

After leaving Condacia, we were destitute of provisions for three days, the country being in a manner eaten up: the usual allowance of rum was still served out, however—-but empty stomachs and ardent spirits do not agree well together; in short, a moderate quantity was sufficient to render a person intoxicated, and this was the case with the most of us. The enemy were also reduced to such straits for meat, that they were obliged to feed on ass and horse flesh; the skins of the asses were often to be seen lying on the road, and the carcass of almost every dead horse we passed by had either one or both hips cut of: to judge by appearance, that part of the horse must be the most savoury—none of us, however, knew by experience.

Coming up one night with the enemy's rear, the light division of our army engaged them, but they retired precipitately over the River Ceira, blowing up the bridge, to stop the pursuit; a number of the enemy, who were still on it, lost their lives in consequence of the explosion being performed too hastily. That night we saw a number of asses which had been hamstrung: if they had not been suffering excruciating agony, we should have been tempted to laugh at the droll contortions of the poor creatures— they lay huddled together among some mud, and whenever any person approached, a general kicking and sprawling took place.

In bivouacking at this place, we had to endure the combined miseries of a wet night and hunger. Next morning, one of the men who had been foraging brought in a bag of Indian corn: with this inestimable treasure he generously went round the whole company, giving each of us a handful. Soon after this, three days' allowance of beef was served out, which quickly restored hilarity, and kept the cooks and jaws hard at work for the remainder of the day.

The blowing up of the bridge had retarded our advance for two days; but on a ford being discovered, we crossed the river on the 17th of March, and continued our march for two successive days. We then halted again, for the ostensible purpose of refreshing ourselves: the word was rather misplaced, considering that we had nothing to eat—it being pretty generally allowed, that meat constitutes no inconsiderable part of refreshment to hungry men. About this time, we were regaled by Lord Wellington reviewing us.

Any little savings the men had made were now obliged to be thrown away in purchasing something to stay the gnawing of their stomachs—often have I seen a private pay a dollar for a small biscuit, thinking himself happy to get it at any price. This time enabled the butchers of the army to reap a golden harvest, they having the offals of all the bullocks they slew as perquisites: the most nauseating garbage was sold at enormous prices. The greasy rogues, knowing their power, held tenaciously at the prices they had laid down; and rather than do otherwise, they would sometimes actually go and bury the carrion underground.

Many of the men were detected here in stealing honey from some hives in the neighbourhood; the colonel discovered the thieves by looking for all those who had their faces stung by the bees: the culprits were punished by extra pickets, or a temporary stoppage of their rum:—but surely it should have been recollected that necessity is all-powerful.

Continuing our march through the north of Portugal, we began to observe that the country was getting more and more barren, and that every house was in a state of beastly filth. Happening to be billeted on a house along with some others, its loathsome Augean-stable-like appearance had nearly saved the inmates the trouble of entertaining us: however, concealing our disgust as much as possible, in the same manner as the wolf did in the ape's den, we entered.

Stepping towards the fireplace to dress our victuals, the black ferocious-looking landlord called to us not to set our feet upon his mother: astonished at this warning, no person being apparently in sight of that description, we looked round more particularly, and discovered something in the form of a human being lying crumpled up in the corner of the ash-pit, which was a step lower than the floor: it was with great difficulty we could believe that it was one of our own species before our eyes, she actually being little larger than a full-grown hen! The host told us that she had lain for upwards of thirty years in the ash-pit, nearly in the same position; age, therefore, not a dwarfish nature, had reduced the creature to a diminutive size, and the strange attitude undoubtedly had materially helped to effect the same. After this time, having no wish to intrude on the privacies of such people, we went out of doors and cooked.

Arriving at the village of Salorica, some of the men went out secretly to "search the ground," as it was called:—this practice had of late become very common, although discountenanced by strict commands to the contrary; but, with regard to this party, they had not searched long till they came upon a jar:—thinking, of course, that it would, without doubt, contain money, the sages unanimously agreed not to lift the treasure till the shades of night should allow them to do so with more security. Marking the place therefore, they returned, planning likely as much future happiness as the barber's brother in the *Arabian Nights*.

The discovery was too important, however, to allow them to be mute; through this means an additional partner to the enterprise was obtained. It seems that a sergeant, remarkable in the regiment only for his low cunning, had overheard their golden discourse; and no sooner had the treasure-seekers sallied forth, at the time agreed on, than he followed on tiptoe, taking the utmost care not to disturb them until the precious jar was disinterred, and fully exposed to the greedy gaze of their wondering eyes—then indeed he stept forward, with a benevolent smile on his countenance, and modestly claimed only two or three shares of what was found.

The party were at first rather disconcerted at the unexpected honour of a visit from a non-commissioned officer on such, an errand; but considering that there still would be enough to make them all, they bore up under the misfortune with some equanimity. But who can describe their sensations when the jar was. uncorked, to find that it only contained some fine olive-oil:—perhaps the tearing of hair, the gnashing of teeth, and cursing the hour of their birth, did not ensue—but the woe of the horror-struck, crew was great.

Envious fortune, however, had not yet expended her quiver of misfortunes—as, at the very time they thought their misery was wound, up to the highest pitch, they were suddenly surprised and taken prisoners, by a sergeant who had orders to look out for all "proggers." The cunning, sergeant was disgraced for this offence, by being reduced to the ranks, notwithstanding his protestations of innocence. One of the excuses was, that he was not of the party; but this defence did not pass, as he found he had over-reached himself for once.

In the course of this march, we had another example of villainous hypocrisy—a sergeant having very officiously found fault with a man for pilfering a little flour from a Portuguese family: he lectured the culprit in the severest terms, upon the heinous sin of plundering the poor starving people: "You should," said he, "rather have given them a portion of your own provisions, than have been so base-minded as to rob them of their last morsel." This was all very well, everyone concurring heartily in the honourable sentiments of the worthy sergeant; and already he was set down as a very saint among us but what was our surprise, on resuming our march, to see the canteen strap of the man of stripes break by accident, and discover to our astonished eyes the identical flour pouring out on the road.

Not daring to charge him openly with the gross deceit, loud murmurings were heard on every side, repeating his very words, such as, "you should have given, and not robbed," &c. The hypocrite, on hearing the just reproof, slunk aside, without saying a single syllable, knowing well what was meant. Thus, it appeared, that the moment the original thief had put back the flour to the place from whence it was taken, our worthy had gone and stolen it himself: I should have said before, that had ordered the man to return the flour to the injured people.

Leaving Portugal we entered Spain, and soon after arrived at the town of Albergeria: a visible change for the better took place in the appearance of the country, the houses, and the people; immediately after crossing the frontiers. The war had raised the price of some articles to an enormous pitch at this place; common salt, for instance, sold at 3s. a pound, and tobacco at 7s.; other things in proportion.

The arrival of the commissary with provisions was at all times looked for as an, event of the last importance; he having to go as far as Lisbon for these necessaries, of course the farther we receded from the coast, the farther were his journeys, and longer the time occupied in performing them. A plain extended for some leagues round the town of Albergeria; and often did we watch to catch the first glimpse of the provision mules. When they did arrive, the very brutes appeared of consequence in our eyes; but the commissary was considered almost as an angel of light. Such are the effects of spare diet upon the minds of hungry men!

Having frequent dealings in the marketplace with the Spanish hucksters, we often had our risibility excited by the rogueries of a long lean Irishman belonging the regiment. This fellow, finding the Spaniards apt to be easily gulled, immediately made proposals to sell their articles for them to us, under the plausible pretext of seeing justice done to both sides—His services were accepted by which means he contrived to cheat the, unsuspecting people every day of a good round sum of money, besides receiving a handsome commission for his trouble.

From the gay deceiver's odd appearance, the Spaniards nicknamed him *Pacalarga*, which, literally translated, means *long-straw*. The whole time we lay in the place, Pacalarga carried on his pranks with such secrecy and success, that scarcely a bargain could be concluded upon, without, his advice being first taken by the honest Albergerians.

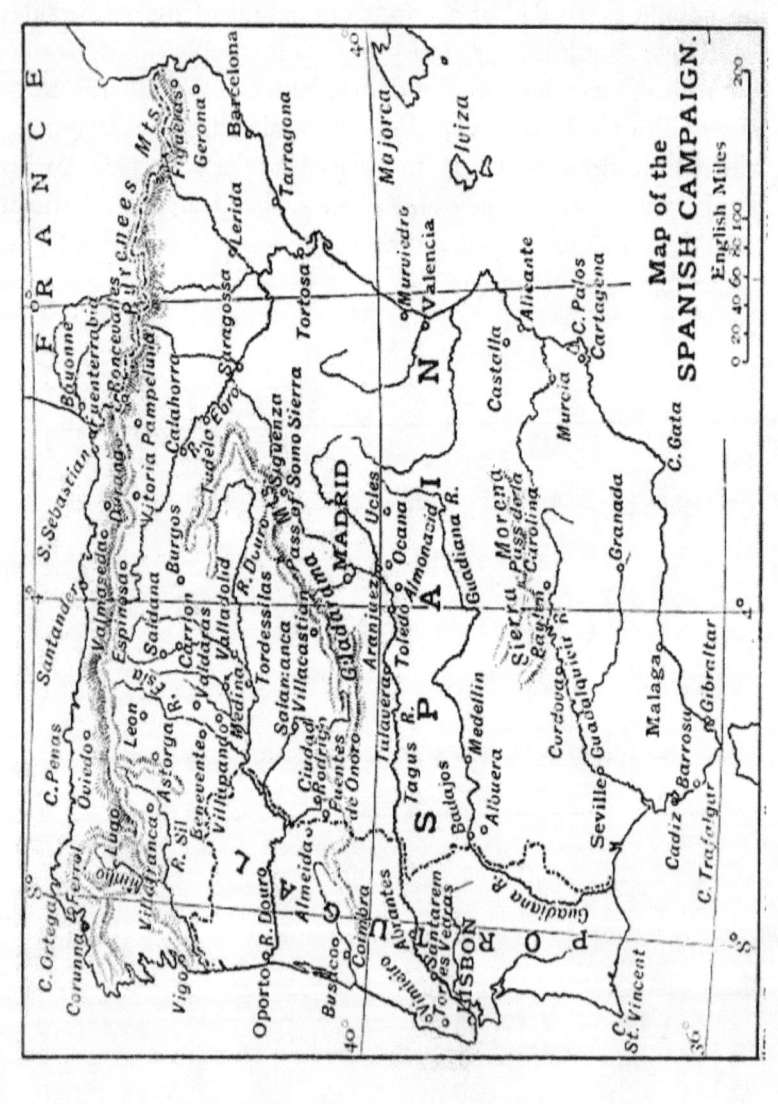

Chapter 5

Harassing March to the Field of Albuhera

The enemy having resumed the offensive, we quitted, our cantonment, and arrived on the plains of Fuentes de Honoro on the 3rd of May a part of our army had already come in contact with, the foe, but we were employed at first only in manoeuvring. This kind of labour was held in universal detestation by the men; principally on account of never seeing any advantage arise from it. Passing over a field of garlic in one of our many tacks, some of the men thought proper to regale themselves on this loathsome vegetable, and their comrades were in a short time almost suffocated with the smell of their breaths.

This caused the garlic-eaters to be assailed with many oaths and curses; but threatening sorts of words are so commonplace among soldiers, that all their terrors are regarded as little as the "playful zephyrs." Permission was at length given for us to stretch our wearied limbs upon the ground: the officers then went out a short distance, to have a nearer view of the engagement going on!

We were soon roused, by the coming up of General Spenser with orders for us to advance to the scene of action. "Come, my lads," said Colonel Cadogan, "you are to get biscuit and rum served out in that village;" concluding the speech thus, in his own peculiar laconic manner. Three men out of each company in the regiment were at this time assisting the wounded of the engaged regiments; they had left their arms and accoutrements behind; we were therefore necessitated to divide, and carry, them, forward by turns.

The old treasure-seeking *ci-devant* sergeant, and, myself had for our share of the luggage a heavy knapsack between us. As we were rapidly approaching the enemy, they opened a fire upon us from some pieces of cannon; one of the balls struck the ground a yard or two to the right of our company, going in such a direction that it was very near sweeping the whole of us down. Arriving at the village of Fuentes, we saw twelve light companies which had been repeatedly driven out of it by the enemy, though they had displayed prodigious valour. The musquetry of the French began already to be felt among us, several of the men falling down wounded.

At a time like this, the bearing of an extra knapsack being an insupportable annoyance to us two, we inquired, of an officer what was to be done with it: "Carry it still, to be sure," was the reply. This being infinitely easier said than done, the old sergeant advised me to join him in throwing it away; I agreed at once to the proposal; and we accordingly pitched it a good distance to the rear. The officer chancing to observe this instance of contempt of his authority, threatened terrible things; but to his menaces we were perfectly indifferent: for what does a man care about the chance of punishment, when the next instant may be his last?

We were preparing to load our musquets, when Cadogan called out, "No loading; an inch of steel is worth a dozen of rounds." Just at this time, the old sergeant was eased of his own knapsack also, in the most miraculous manner, a cannon-ball having very politely come and cut it clean off his back, without doing him the slightest injury! Our customary salute of three cheers was now given; the bagpipes struck up a warlike *pibroch*, and suddenly we rushed down the village street, and took in an instant 100 men and 10 officers prisoners.

We next crossed a small rivulet in our way, then recrossed it, skirmishing all the while; and continuing to do so, till Night, as if in compassion to foolish men, threw her sable mantle over the earth. Our regiment had thus the merit of being the first that lodged itself in the village of Fuentes de Honoro, but, as might be expected, all this honour could not be purchased without blood; two of our officers were mortally wounded, another received a severe thrust from a bayonet, and several of the privates were killed and wounded.

But I return to a more humble theme, to wit, food; two days had already elapsed since the smallest morsel had passed our lips: this would, perhaps, have been nothing, to old musty knights-errant, and may be regarded as little even by the reader. We now felt the pangs of hunger to an indescribable degree. In fact, this was the case with the whole brigade we belonged to; while, at the very same time, it was notorious to us all, that the regiments of guards had their haversacks full of bread: these fellows were at all times better supplied, and more care taken of their precious persons, to keep them from any unnecessary danger or fatigue, than any of the regiments of the line. This night, however, orders were despatched to them to deliver, up as much bread as would supply the whole of us with a quarter of a pound to each man; this was received accordingly.

Meanwhile, to prevent a surprise, the most of the men bivouacked in the street. The place being completely deserted by the inhabitants, in rummaging through the houses we procured some flour a stray pig was also discovered. The man who was employed to kill, it not being very expert at the business, the animal ran off after receiving the first stab of his bayonet; this obliged him to commence a hot pursuit, making many a clumsy thrust, to our great diversion. Cadogan observing the affair, gave the awkward butcher some hearty curses, and ordered him to pin it to the ground; this he at length accomplished; and soon gave the unfortunate porker the *coup de grâce*. Sleep was at this time totally disregarded, the whole night being devoted to the baking of flour-cakes.

Next morning the French commenced firing at us: we were ordered not to return it, but to go down to the edge of the river and lie under cover. Here we lay snug enough, but; as in the fable of the boys and frogs, no sooner did we venture to put up our heads, than a shower of balls would whistle past us. This was rather a provoking predicament to be in; especially as we were all burning with thirst, and the river was tunning close by us. One of the men, either unable to wait longer without drinking, or wishing to shew his courage jumped hastily up and ran down to the river, filled his canteen, find came back safe and sound, contrary to our expectation; the enemy, meanwhile, sending their bullets about his ears like hail.

The moment our gentleman arrived, he uncorked his canteen with a triumphant air, saying, at the same time, he would now let us all drink; but lo! what was his surprise, on opening it, not to find any water within—a bullet, having pierced the side of the canteen, had allowed every drop to escape. At this adventure, although our tongues nearly clove to our throats, we could not resist the impulse of bursting out into aloud laugh—so ludicrously blank was the countenance of the water-carrier, who prudently declined risking his life a second time.

A flag of truce came from the enemy, for permission to bury their dead and carry off their wounded. The request being granted, we took the opportunity of doing the same services to our own fallen comrades; in consequence of this, the remainder of the day continued quiet. To secure ourselves from any sudden surprise, we took the precaution of slightly barricading the streets with loose stones. At night I returned to the house where I had been before, and found that four sides of bacon had been discovered in my absence: this, with the addition of a bag of salt, which I had the honour of finding, formed a mess which, as the saying, is, was fit for a prince.

Next morning, the, enemy, being firmly determined upon, obtaining possession of the village, they attached that part of our army which was posted to the right of us., Having succeeded in compelling them to retreat, the French now advanced upon us. Not calculating upon, being thus flanked, the whole, regiment was, dispersed throughout the streets and houses of the village, in expectation that the enemy must needs cross the river before coming at us. Lulled into security by this means, we were suddenly surprised by the entrance of the French on the right; the rest of them, then crossed the river, and broke furiously through the barricades.

Surrounded thus on all sides, and, finding it useless to withstand, in our disordered state, the attack of the numerous force which was pouring into the town. We thought it no disgrace to take to our heels: I must confess, that our flight had something the appearance of rabbits running from their holes. All of us succeeded in gaining the outside of the village, with the exception of half a company, who were hemmed in and taken prisoners, among which was Rae, the old Paisley Methodist.

No sooner had we formed our *pêle-mêle* ranks into good array, than the French emerged from the village, and drew up opposite to us, within musket shot. We proceeded immediately to open a scattering fire upon them; the 74th and 88th regiments then advanced to our relief; and instantly poured in such a terrific volley upon their ranks, that the fall of a long wall may be aptly compared to the ranks that fell; and the loss was the more important to the enemy, as those killed were chiefly grenadiers. We still continued giving and receiving a constant fire; but our ammunition running short, some of us went a little to the rear for a fresh supply: at this moment General Nightingale rode up to our party, and said, that as we had had plenty of fighting already, we might remain where we were.

Most people will think; this was a very polite offer—so we thought also, but as we knew that the rest of our regiment, along with others, was at the very time preparing to charge, it was natural enough for us to be chagrined a little at not being allowed to participate in the approaching honour, whatever it might be. One of the men set us an example how to act, by running suddenly forward towards the regiment: the general, enraged at this disobedience of his orders, cried, "Stop him!"—the words had scarcely fallen from his lips; when a cannon-ball passed so close to the fugitive as to make him wheel round by the wind of it; passing on then, it nearly grazed the head of, the general's horse.

I was now aroused myself by the cries of *bomba.*, and *courez*, from a Portuguese regiment which lay under cover near us: on looking round, I found that the warnings were addressed to me, a shell having alighted unperceived at my feet; happily, I had time to make a precipitate retreat before it burst.

The heat of battle, and the confusion, enabled us to join, the regiment, without any further opposition being made to our wishes. We were just in time to join in the charge made upon the French with the bayonet: they were once more driven through the village. The light brigade now came to relieve us; but the fight was completely ended—chiefly through the interposition of night. This concluded the Battle of Fuentes de Honoro. Our loss in the divers engagements on the 3rd and 5th was heavy, amounting to about 200 men and 10 officers, killed, wounded, and prisoners.

The author of *Don Roderick* has deigned to notice some events in this battle, in the following lines:—

> *And what avails thee that, for Cameron slain.*
> *Wild from his plaided ranks the yell was given—*
> *Vengeance and grief gave mountain rage the rein,* &c.
> The gallant Col. Cameron was wounded—mortally during the desperate contest in the streets of the village called Fuentes de Honoro. He fell at the head of his native Highlanders, the 71st and 79th, who raised a dreadful shriek of grief and rage.

Several egregious errors are contained in the above words. Either Sir Walter has been misinformed, or he has taken upon himself a vast stretch of poetical license, He has made the 71st all "native Highlanders;" whereas, to say that there were forty or fifty of them in the whole regiment, would, perhaps, overrate the real number. The proportion of Lowlanders in the 79th was not so great; still there was no small quantity of them in that regiment. Sir Walter has made the 71st yell, shriek, and grieve, at the fall of a man who was an entire stranger to them. I can assure him that such demonstrations of woe were never shewn by any of us. I cannot think, either, that there could be much yelling. On this occasion among the 79th, the alleged cause of it being a

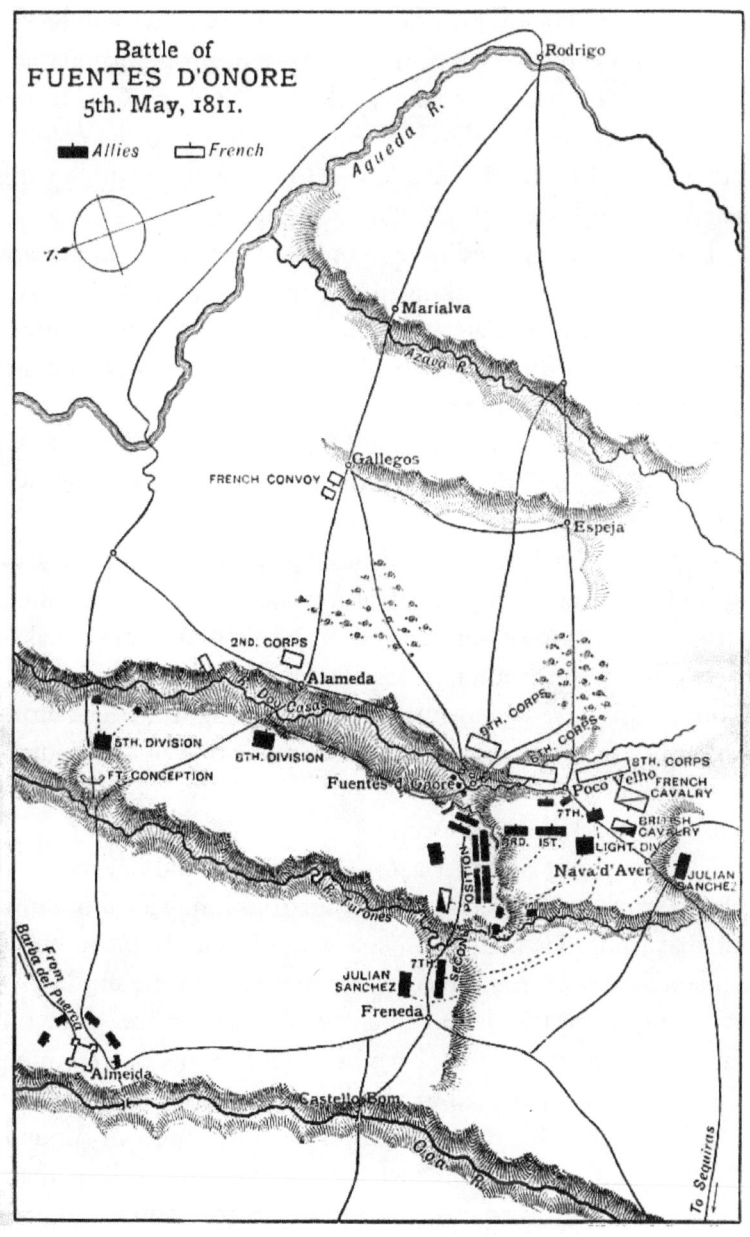

complete martinet in practice and disposition, and consequently not precisely the idol of the men.

Among the French prisoners taken at Fuentes, we recognised a Swiss who had deserted from us at the retreat of Corunna, and who, it appears, had gone back to the French again. One of our sergeants had the coldblooded cruelty to go up to the colonel, and inquire if he might be allowed to shoot the man; but this brutal, proposal was rejected with abhorrence.

Two days were, passed over in the field of battle, without any important occurrence taking place, the hostile armies merely watching each other. We were not powerful enough to attack the French; and they, on their part, seemed unwilling to come to blows with us. By the retiring of the enemy, we were allowed to return to our old quarters at Albergeria: in performing this journey we crossed that part of the field of Fuentes which was to the right of the village.

Here we found that a good number of men had been slain on both sides; and that the Spanish peasants had stripped them to the skin, instead of burying them. The sight of so many naked corpses huddled together, created feelings of disgust and humiliation: in this state it was impossible to distinguish friend from; foe, Briton from Frenchman, with the exception of one body, of huge dimensions, which, having a long beard, we judged to have belonged to a French pioneer.

The people of Albergeria, on missing their old salesman Pacalarga from among us, made many anxious inquiries about him; but that righteous man had been wounded, and sent home to England. We were, reinforced at our present cantonment by two companies from the depot; I believe if it had not been for this timely succour we should, have been sent home, our regiment being so much weakened in numbers.

It was about this time that the French garrison of Almeida effected their escape from that fortress in such a gallant manner, although it was environed round by British and Portuguese troops: I believe the noise of the cannonading in this affair was heard in our quarters. Little or no blame could be attached to any particular part of the besieging army for this seeming negligence; fate, circumstances, or the ability of the enemy's general, may at times deceive the most wary, as one or more of these causes did in this case. However, one of those vulgar rhymes which nobody makes, but which is in the mouth of every one, was raised on this occasion: for the insertion of it I hope I may be pardoned:—

> *The lions went to sleep,*
> *The lambs went to play.*
> *And out of Almeida*
> *The French marched away.*

To explain this hobbling verse, it is necessary to say, that the 2nd and 4th, two of the implicated regiments, had for their ensigns or mottos a sphynx or lamia, and a lion: the 2nd obtained the former sign on account of the part they bore in the Egyptian expedition. It will be seen, on inspecting the foregoing distich, that by a transition as rapid as any in Ovid's *Metamorphoses*, the lamia is converted into a lamb.

Intelligence having arrived that a French Army, under the command of Marshal Soult, was advancing from Andalusia to relieve Badajoz, which was invested by Beresford's Allied Army of British, Portuguese, and Spaniards, our brigade, consisting of the 60th, 71st, and 92nd regiments, accordingly received orders to march to their assistance. The exigency of the case demanding speed, we hastily broke up our quarters, and commenced our march southwards at the unusual hour of seven in the evening: intense darkness coming on soon after, the whole regiment and two companies of the 92nd were separated from the rest.

The whole night was passed going to and fro, endeavouring to grope our way in this unknown part of the country, till daybreak length shewed that we were only six miles distant from the original place of starting. Galling as this discovery was, we hurried on; and, by dint of much sweat and toil, overtook the other part of the brigade by noon. A very short time was allowed us for the purpose of refreshing ourselves. On we went again, as quickly as possible; but the intense heat of the day, united to the fatigue, almost overpowered many a panting, way-worn straggler. Joyfully did we halt at ten o'clock in the evening, having achieved a march of twenty-seven hours almost without any intermission of repose.

For some days we continued to advance with the utmost speed, although not with the murderous rapidity of the first day's journey; and crossing the Tagus at Villa Velha, we arrived and joined the Allied Army on the field of Albuhera. To our astonishment, we learned that the bloody battle bearing that name had been fought some time previous to our arrival; thus, doing away with, or rendering useless, the painful march that we had undergone.

I have no right to describe an engagement which I did not see. The tremendous slaughter on both sides, the murderous effects of the charge of the enemy's lancers on our men, and the reduction of the 3rd regiment, or Buffs, from 800 men to 40, are facts already well known. It was foolish for either British or French to claim the victory on this occasion, their loss being evidently equal, and neither party having cause to boast of any advantage. To give an idea of the mangled appearance of our troops, I may give the report of a 71st man, who was among the first that saw them. "I saw," said he, "five or six regiments sitting under a tree!" It is understood that this account was rather exaggerated.

On our first entrance on the field of slaughter, a heavy, nauseous smell assailed our nostrils: this was partly caused by the immense number of dead lying buried under ground, and partly by the fleshy fuel of the fires, with which it was found necessary to expedite the extermination of those bodies which the already gorged ground was unable to take into its cold maw. The carcasses of both men and horses were thus dragged into heaps and burned: the black and scorched sites of these sacrifices were still distinctly visible to us, covered with numerous calcined bones.

We were now incorporated with General Hill's little army, and in fact continued so till the end of the war: we had certainly by this means less dangerous fighting at times than Wellington's grand army; but we sustained much greater fatigue, on account of our being employed chiefly as a sort of flying army; but not a cowardly one, be it understood—though the term *flying* is perhaps rather equivocal.

Leaving the remainder of Beresford's troops to join Wellington's, which had come up by this time, we made a sweep round Badajoz, and crossed the Guadiana, the grand army, having invested that place; but having nothing to do with this business, we went on and encamped near Elvas. Here we were visited with one of the heaviest thunder showers I ever recollect to have seen or felt; a few minutes after its commencement, we found ourselves lying as it were in the bed of a running stream; but such a bed not being exactly to our taste, we hastily broke down a number of branches from the neighbouring trees, with the intention of stretching our limbs upon them for the rest of the night. This contrivance succeeded pretty well, the water rushing under these little bridges, without doing us much injury. Passing through Elvas, we took up another encampment at Toro de Moro, situated within a short distance of Campo Mayor.

No immediate prospect of business in our way being at hand, we were employed in constructing huts covered with broom, to keep ourselves in a more comfortable state than tents could effect, and at the same time to shield off the rays of the burning summer sun. The powerful fervency of that luminary soon withering our broomy roofs, we were constrained continually to repair them, which in such weather was no small labour. Colonel Cadogan had a fine large hut built for himself, surrounded by walks and shrubbery; and the altering, mending, pruning, and beautifying of this rustic palace gave continual employment to a number of the men. This sort of toil was sorely grudged by them, it being considered entirely unnecessary.

One day, as Cadogan sat in his hut, the unwilling labourers began to revile and curse him amongst themselves for giving them so much trouble: little did they know that the object upon which they were expending their wrath was close by at the time. Although every word of the abuse rung in Cadogan's ears, he had too much magnanimity to get into a rage, or even to take notice of it at the time. This, I believe, was exactly the same conduct that the celebrated French General Turenne pursued when placed in a similar predicament. Hearing that a draft of 350 recruits from the depot had landed at Lisbon, and were coming up to join us, Cadogan gave us orders to build huts for them; saying, at the same time, "See that there is no grumbling among them; I heard what you said of me the other day; remember that we are not in Glasgow barracks." The recruits had inadvertently devoured such quantities of fruit and other garbage on the road from Lisbon, that on their arrival a severe flux attacked them, by which a good number died.

Our time of relaxation in this camp was the forenoon: we had liberty to lie in the huts during the heat of the day, and the privilege of bathing in a river which ran at no great distance from our dwellings. While laving our limbs in the crystal wave, it was no difficult task to distinguish those who had lately arrived in the country, by the superior whiteness of their skins: our own had now become, nearly as brown as a fox's; in fact, the skin was such an invariable criterion, that the length of time a person had remained in the Peninsula could be told by it within a few months. On these occasions of bathing, we had often an opportunity of admiring the dexterity of the Portuguese soldiers in diving; they would remain for an astonishing length of time under water, and contrive to catch and bring up a number of fishes.

The river I have mentioned is, like most other peninsular ones, infested by numbers of water snakes and leeches: they never harmed us, however, I cannot say so much for the land serpents, at least if striking terror can be accounted a cause of complaint. An Irishman belonging to the regiment was out one day washing his shirt, and having accomplished this, the process of drying it next took place: this necessary operation of course requiring some little time, Pat must needs do something to relieve his *ennui*; espying a serpent lying close by, basking itself in the sun, he attacked it with a *shillelagh*; but the poor descendant of the old Eden deceiver was not at all disposed to encourage such striking attentions; on the contrary, it darted with the greatest fury at our hero, who, no longer willing to continue the conflict, wisely took to his heels, leaving his only shirt behind: the vindictive creature gave him chase nearly to the very camp, making many leaps, before it relinquished the pursuit.

Pat was so terrified, that some of us had to go along with him, as a sort of escort, to fetch back the shirt. At another time, while we were upon the march, a serpent was discovered stretched out on the middle of the road: one of the men aimed a blow at it with the but-end of his firelock; but missing his mark, it was preparing to fly at him, when an officer drew his sword and cut it in two.

Wellington's grand army had, ere this time, been obliged to abandon the siege of Badajoz, and take refuge within the frontiers of Portugal, in consequence of the junction of the armies of Marmont and Soult, the aggregate number of which was considered too powerful to contend with. The whole of Spain being thus again under the control of the enemy, measures were taken to prevent their entrance into Portugal; Wellington taking up a position on the north, or Beira side of the Tagus, while our little army received orders to do the same on the south, or Alentejo side of that river. Leaving, therefore, the camp of Toro de Moro, after a residence of six weeks there, we marched to the town of Borba.

The French never having penetrated into this part of the kingdom, we found the inhabitants in as primitive and tranquil a state as if profound peace had reigned for centuries in the Peninsula. Having escaped the contamination of warlike horrors, the manners and customs of the nation were seen here in greater purity than in the north.

One day, acting as orderly to Colonel Cadogan, I found him lodged in a large genteel house. While I was dancing attendance at this place, his groom-boy, a Catholic, invited me, by way of a great favour, to go and see the lady of the house at her devotions. I went accordingly, and, on looking into a splendid room, beheld, the lady kneeling before an image of the Virgin, praying with the utmost fervency, and at times offering it a cup of water. Many of the Portuguese were to be seen going about the streets at night, playing on guitars, and accompanying the music with their voices. The general term given to this custom is serenading, I understand; but I never saw them performing under the window of a favourite *dulcinea*, as the common acceptation of the word implies.

One of the German hussars in our service met his death here by accident: he was in a sickly state, and had gone down to the side of a well to drink; in doing this it was supposed that he had fallen into it; at any rate he was found drowned: accordingly, his countrymen buried him with military honours. While they were firing over the grave, a Portuguese woman, who was looking at the ceremony, inquired seriously of us, how long the man would be in going home? or, to use her manner of expressing it, how long he would be in crossing "*La Mar?*" It would appear by this, that she had an idea that Protestants consider death as only a kind of passport for their own country;—a similar opinion is held by the negroes. One of the men, well aware how useless it was to combat with bigoted prejudice, answered that the German would be "three days in going home."

Apparently, the zeal of the Portuguese in the common cause was not so high as might have been expected; their authorities being obliged to have recourse to the impressment of soldiers, in the same manner as in our enlightened country we procure seamen. It was common enough to see strings of forty men driven into the town like flocks of geese; they were all tied to each other as a security for their honour. The general costume of these recruits was knee-breeches and naked legs, along with the invariable *sombrero*: as for the other parts of their raiment, the genius of raggedness forbids any description but, in the words, "things of shreds and patches"—the only account that comes near the truth.

The scowling eyes and dusky visages of these fellows, or rather their *tout ensemble*, had a very brigand appearance. Their escort, or drivers, were generally old men, armed with rusty bayonets fastened to the ends of poles, others had guns without locks, and the like formidable weapons.

In common with other southern nations, the Portuguese have an aversion to the use of ardent spirits: although their soldiers received exactly the same allowance of every article as ourselves, yet they often came to us and exchanged their rum for biscuits. Honest enough customers for the rum were certainly found among us—-but there were some thirsty rogues also, who contrived to cheat the unsuspecting Portuguese out of a good deal of liquor; they having a polite custom of asking us to taste it out of their horns before a bargain was concluded.

By this means, the mere tasters always outnumbered the buyers; and special care was taken by them not to say a word till a hearty pull was obtained from the horn; then the rum was sure to be bad or watered, and an affectation made of spitting it out with disgust. In this manner, every horn that came in their reach was pretty sure to be nearly emptied of its contents. Many of the fellows got drunk upon the "*pruevas*," that being the name the Portuguese gave the trying of the liquor; *prueva*, or proof, having the same meaning.

We left the town of Borba on an excessive hot morning, the scorching sun beating on our heads with prodigious force. This, in conjunction with a total want of water, caused many to hang out their parched tongues, while others fell powerless to the ground, unable to proceed. As was done to myself on a former occasion, the officers went about persuading the fallen men to get up and move on. A strange manner of persuasion was adopted by the Highland officer who had reproved our impiety at the nunnery in such elevated terms: "Rise up," said he, "I ken you are a strong man by your hough:" the panting object of his attention was unable to do much more than smile at this uncouth address.

But to return to the subject, the whole of the men came into the halting place in small straggling parties; I was among the first to reach it—the major part not arriving till the cool of the evening. The effects of this day's march were the putting of 300 men into the hospital, seriously injured in health: they of course belonged to different regiments of the brigade.

Next day we marched to Portalegre. The grand army had about this time made an incursion into Spain and laid siege to Ciudad Rodrigo; but they retraced their steps into Portugal again, on the approach of Marmont's army to its relief.

CHAPTER 6

Covering of the Siege of Badajoz

Having for some time escaped any dangerous service, while our other army was suffering some of its hardships, we were at length roused from our languor, by orders arriving from Wellington. We, together with some Spanish troops, were to drive General Girard's army out of Estremadura; they having been lording it over that province for some time.

Issuing forth, accordingly, from Portalegre with great alacrity on the 22nd of October, we marched with the utmost rapidity for four successive days. We entered Spain, passing through Alburquerque and Aliseda: at the latter place we were joined by the Spanish allies. The velocity of our advance soon leaving the provision waggons far behind, we were at one time obliged to make an attack on a large cabbage-field along with the starving horses and mules: however, we put the cabbages through the operation of boiling before feeding on them—and miserable cheer they were, after all.

Meanwhile, the enemy, informed of our movements, continued to retreat before us: about this time, however, he seemed to have been thrown off his guard, as we guessed by his pace slackening by degrees, and his halt at Arroyo Molinos. Due information of these circumstances reaching us, we pursued our weary way, in despite of bad roads and heavy rain, till we arrived within two leagues of the place. Having halted, and got some rice served out, we waited impatiently till darkness would allow us to carry our project of surprising the enemy into execution: the continuance of the wind and rain, without having permission to kindle fires, no doubt increased our wish to terminate the business as soon as possible.

At two o'clock in the morning of the 28th October we started silently for the place of destination, wading amidst the muddy mountain roads in the dark till daylight broke; it was then discovered that Arroyo Molinos was in sight; and being on arising ground, the better to escape observation, the whole army descended into a hollow. While in this situation, we saw a Spanish peasant come out of the town and commence his agricultural labours in a field, without observing that thousands of armed men were close by him.

Part of the army, under the command of General Howard, was now ordered to make a circle round the town, in order to prevent the enemy's retreat; another portion, including our regiment, was instructed to advance directly on the town. Presently, the busy sound of examining flints and tying down chin-straps was heard—the certain indications of an approaching brush. All these necessary preparations being accomplished, General Hill gave the word of command—"Shoulder arms." When that was done, he said, "Move on, my lads, and *God be with you!*" Just at the time, a tremendous shower of rain came on, which, although it wet our skins, did not *damp* our courage—the secrecy of the enterprise being rather favoured than otherwise by the cloudy discharge.

When we reached the outskirts of the place, a picket of French cavalry was discovered in an olive wood, squatting round some fires, with their horses tied to the trees:—they had apparently retired to this shelter in consequence of the shower, perhaps not many minutes before our arrival—so much, as some folks would say, had Providence favoured us. Fearful of disturbing the cavalry, lest they should escape, and spread the alarm of our approach, we marched cautiously by, while they were lulled into such security that not one of them perceived us. Leaving a company to surprise them, we pushed on, and entered the town without opposition.

Early as it was, the French were at the same time marching

out of the town, on the opposite side from whence we were, totally unconscious, however, of our presence; but there was still a good number of them in and about the houses. Meanwhile, we advanced along with the 92nd, according to orders, without stopping or firing a shot; the 50th following close behind, securing the prisoners as they ran distractedly out of the houses. An interesting object now drew our attention—it was one of the French commanders, Prince d'Aremberg, running out with a coffee cup in his hand—alarm and astonishment strongly depicted on his countenance, at the arrival of such uninvited visitors, and at the joyous shouts with which we made the welkin ring.

Little time was allowed for his amazement to subside: scarce an instant elapsed till the epaulets and other frippery were plucked from his person by some of the men; he was also rather roughly treated, being shoved about from side to side, in order to compel him to join in the noisy cheering: this request was at length complied with by the poor man, but with great reluctance, and endeavours to let it be known that he was a "principe." To save himself from further ill usage, he then threw himself into the arms of an officer in hopes of protection—but was rudely thrust away by this gentleman, who should have known better: however, men in the heat of a confusion such as this, may be hurried into actions which they will blush for at a cooler moment.

Continuing our course through the town, we met the body of French cavalry direct in the teeth, who had been dislodged from the wood at the first outset of the affair; they had fled by a circuitous route, and thus came unexpectedly upon us. Seeing no other means of escape but that of forcing through us, they charged with the fury of despair: unfortunately, our musquets were in such a state, on account of the late rains, that few or none of them would give fire; this encouraged the horsemen, they being now intermixed with us, hewing and cutting on all sides; some of them penetrated to the place where Colonel Cadogan was: a blow aimed at him divided his cap in two, but, happily, the sword glanced off without doing any real injury.

The Marquess of Tweeddale, and a Major Churchill, perceiving the colonel's imminent danger, immediately rode up and cut down the assailant, at the same time completely dispersing the others We had ere this betaken ourselves to the trusty bayonet; one of the men had driven his with such force into the body of a horse, that the animal, writhing with pain, made a sudden jerk, and ran off a good distance, with both musquet and bayonet sticking in its side, the rider being unable to stop its furious course: the owner of the arms soon afterwards recovered them. At length the horsemen were overcome by numbers, and either all killed or taken prisoners: their bravery was the admiration of the men, although it was to our cost, several of our soldiers being slain or wounded. The whole time the contest was going on, the Spanish inhabitants were looking on, and shouting "success to the red coats," in their own language.

This last obstacle surmounted, we passed on to the end of the town without further obstruction; here the remainder of the enemy were drawn up in a wavering state, uncertain whether, to fight or fly; this suspense was soon settled by our opening on them a destructive fire,, while the Portuguese artillery commenced playing upon their ranks with appalling havoc; panic overpowered them, and suddenly some of the French flung down their arms and fled; the rest, keeping up as much appearance of order as their situation would admit, immediately commenced a precipitate retreat.

This was promptly baulked by the appearance of General Howard's troops in the path: the enemy were thus nearly enclosed on all sides; terror and surprise caused every restraint to be abandoned, and irretrievable confusion took place amongst them: " save himself who can," was the order of the day, and happy was he who gained the summit of the neighbouring lofty hills. Others took to flight along the road; but on all sides they were hotly pursued by the Spanish cavalry and infantry, along with such of the British and Portuguese as were not yet exhausted with fatigue.

Such a complete victory as this seldom occurs, nearly the

one half of the enemy's army being taken prisoners, amounting to little short of 2,000 men, including the Prince d'Aremberg, General Brun, and many other officers; the rest of the trophies were, the whole of the enemy's artillery, magazines of corn, baggage, and even some money which had been forced from the Spaniards under the name of a contribution.

The Battle of Arroyo Molinos, small as it was, comparatively speaking, may be said to have been the first decided advantage the British obtained in this war; it was the first instance, at any rate, in which they had acted upon the offensive, and its results were splendid, unlike those "of our former engagements."

Leaving Molinos, we advanced to Merida, and afterwards returned to Portalegre. In December following, intelligence arriving that a French Army under Dombrowski was ravaging Estremadura, our army received orders to enter that province, in order to chastise or expel the invaders. Having marched so far on our way, we came unexpectedly on a party of 300 French busily employed cooking; these men no sooner descried us, than they hastily started up, formed a square with great presence of mind, and commenced a retreat.

Our cavalry taking the lead, pursued, and made several ineffectual attempts to break them; the gallant little band repulsing the horsemen with great slaughter at every charge. The celerity of the enemy's progress prevented our cannon from making any serious impression, one ball alone taking effect, killing three men and wounding two others.

At one time a company of us were mounted behind the horsemen, with the intention of being carried speedily forward, and set down close by the French, in order to try the effect of infantry, but this scheme was not carried into execution; for, to their honour be it said, the enemy succeeded in reaching Merida in safety, after having kept our whole army at bay for the greater part of a day. During the pursuit, immense flocks of carrion crows hovered over us in seeming expectation of a battle; animal instinct teaching them that abundance of food is to them the result of such an event.

Dombrowski flying precipitately on our approach, we passed through Merida and advanced as far as Villa Franca, scaring and putting to flight another little army under Drouet; then wheeling about, we returned to Portalegre; passing, by the way, the bodies, or rather skeletons of the three Frenchmen who had been slain about eight days before. An anatomist could not have scraped the flesh cleaner off a body than the crows had done off those of these men; the bones looked as if they had been boiled or bleached white. Although the prompt destruction of putrid carcasses be beneficial to the health of the living, yet we hate the destroyer, or, in more common words, "we like the treason but detest the traitor:" the dingy birds were therefore held in abhorrence ever after.

Our late expedition, having cut off the communication of Soult and Marmont's armies, Wellington's army was enabled to lay siege to Ciudad Rodrigo with the greater security. In the beginning of the year 1812 we moved northward to Castella Branca, and met there a number of French prisoners coming from Ciudad Rodrigo; that important fortress having been stormed and captured by our grand army: Two companies of our regiment were detached to Lisbon as an escort to the prisoners; meanwhile the army returned, for the last time, to Portalegre.

On the news of Wellington having invested Badajoz reaching us, we marched towards that place, passing through Albuquerque and crossing Guadiana; by which time we found ourselves in the midst of the besieging army, witnesses and listeners to the terrible fire kept up between them and the French garrison. Parting from the grand army on the evening of the same day, we advanced as far as Don Bonito, our orders being to cover its operations. Although sixty miles distant from Badajoz, we still could hear the roar of the artillery employed in the siege, particularly in the mornings or other calm intervals: perhaps the River Guadiana contributed to carry the sound, that stream running by our quarters, and washing the walls of Badajoz at the same time.

After sojourning in Don Bonito for a week, we fell back on

Merida and blew up a bridge there, in order to stop the progress of Soult's army, which was advancing with the intention of relieving Badajoz. We continued to retire till the flashes of the guns and musquetry engaged in the siege were visible. Soon after-this we received news of the surrender of Badajoz: this event was celebrated among us with the powerful aid of extra rum. Colonel Cadogan stood in front of the regiment, and set an example, by drinking "Success to the British arms," or something to that import: thus, for the first time, Cadogan officiated as a fugleman to his own men.

The successful issue of two sieges, and the subsequent retreat of the enemy's armies, emboldened Wellington to form another project—this was to destroy the bridge of Almaraz, it being the common, thoroughfare between the north and, south of Spain, and thereby considered a post of the greatest consequence. On account of our army having escaped the dangers of Rodrigo and Badajoz, it was thought fit to intrust us with the execution of the scheme. Proceeding, therefore, to Almandralego, where a draft from Britain joined us, we passed through Merida, and marched to Truxillo, where six companies of the men were quartered in Pizarro's house: many changes have taken place in this dwelling; this was another; General Hope and his staff had been lodged in it when we were here in 1808.

Still pursuing our way towards Almaraz, we at one time halted, and were exercised in the duties of escalades, this business being entirely new to us: scaling ladders were placed on each side of the parapets of a bridge, the feet of the ladders resting on the dry bed of the rivulet; whoever then ran up the one side and down on the other in the nimblest manner, was considered the most meritorious. Part of the army was now detached to attack the castle of Mirabete, a fortified, place, perched on an exceeding high mountain, and commanding a pass near Almaraz.

Moving on, then, after our odd, but necessary preliminary instructions in storming, we marched a whole night, in hopes of surprising the enemy betimes; but daylight shewing that the place of destination was still at too great a distance for such an attempt, it was thought requisite, from the state of the roads, to leave the artillery, and ascend a mountainous road; where, as the attack was deferred till the following morning, we were allowed to repose ourselves till night. In a few minutes nearly the whole brigade lay fast asleep, but a sudden cry of "stand to your arms!" made every one start on his feet: on all sides, the noise of fixing bayonets, and other warlike preparations, was heard; such words never being uttered except in cases of imminent danger. It was soon discovered, however, that the alarm had proceeded from one of the men, in his dream. Just as Mercutio says:—

And then dreams he of cutting foreign throaty
Of breaches, ambuscadoes, Spanish blades.

Similar occurrences are not uncommon among military men; I have seen 20,000 men extended on the ground, to all appearance buried in sleep, yet at the slightest alarm or noise of any kind, every one of this large body of men would start up simultaneously, and prepare for action: this was done the more readily if the enemy was in the neighbourhood; in fact, the mind on such occasions is in something of the same state as that of the traveller who has to get up from his couch at a fixed time, and who is consequently in terror of oversleeping himself.

Night now approaching, and the object of our mission being still unperformed, not to speak of a tiresome tramp besides, we marched, or rather clambered off, a company of us carrying a quantity of broom to burn the bridge, and two of the best swimmers in the regiment were in readiness to bring the bridge back, if the enemy attempted to set it adrift; however, these, plans were not carried into effect, for divers reasons. The difficulties of picking our steps through the mountains were much increased by the inky darkness of the night. No paths could be found save those made by the goatherds, these men being-in reality the only human beings who disturbed the solitude of these wilds: their roads, it may be judged, therefore, were not of an unmeasurable breadth; so did we find, as sometimes only one man could pass them at a time: but it is needless to drag the reader along the whole way; it is sufficient to say, that, after having several marvellous escapes from falling over precipices, we descended into a valley on the morning of the 19th of May, and came in sight of the bridge, with all its forts and fortifications.

The enemy being fully apprised of our approach, we were saluted instantly with some cannon-balls from their nearest battery. As time is precious on such occasions, it was thought expedient to employ only the 60th regiment and a wing of ours, as the storming party. They accordingly advanced to the assault, and in a short time placed their ladders against the walls of Fort Napoleon; the remainder of us, along with the 92nd, kept stationary, about a hundred yards from the walls, ready to give support if required. Our comrades were now to be seen mounting the ladders, regardless of the heavy fire which the enemy poured down upon them; the fire was returned from some at the foot of the walls, yet a number of the men were shot or thrust off the ladders with bayonets before an entrance was effected, which was done at length, every opposition being borne down, a 71st man entering the place first of all—a thing very gratifying to us, of course.

Almost at the very instant Fort Napoleon was taken possession of, the enemy began to pour a cannonade into it from Fort Ragusa, on the opposite side of the River Tagus: this precipitation gained them nothing, as a body of their own countrymen were rushing out at the gate, endeavouring to escape the bayonets of our men; they were nearly swept off to a man by this ill-timed fire. The guns of Fort Napoleon were now turned against Ragusa, which in a short time compelled the garrison to consult their safety in flight: and the whole achievement of storming and carrying the fortifications of Almaraz was accomplished in the short space of fifteen minutes.

Liberty was now given to pile arms; and we spectators set off full speed towards the fort, for the purpose of coming in for a share of whatever booty was going: some stingy officers attempted to throw obstructions in the way, but General Hill commanded them to desist, saying, that "we had wrought hard enough for anything which might be obtained." Reaching the desired havens, we found that an interesting scene of noise and confusion was taking place since the din of war had ended; numbers of tame goats were running about on all sides, flying from the men, who were eagerly pursuing them with no friendly intent. It seems, that almost every one of the French garrison had been possessed of a goat or two, either for pets or for their milk, or perhaps for both purposes. Immense magazines of provisions and spirits were also laid open to our attacks—they consisted of rice, biscuits, hams, brandy, &c,: the filling of haversacks and canteens gave employment for some time, in consequence of this God-send.

But a 50th man was the most successful of any, he coming out of some secret place or other with his cap filled with gold *doubloons*: each of these coins is equivalent to 3*l*. 17*s*. sterling; it may be judged, therefore, that a capful of them would constitute a pretty round sum. A 71st man had the good fortune to find a colour belonging to the *corps étranger*; for, to be candid, I must say, that he had not an opportunity of taking it by force of arms—but the difference of the honour is merely ideal; for what, in reality, is the honour of a stained rag?

Having no intention of keeping possession of our conquest, our mission being only to destroy, we set about dismantling the works with great alacrity while some part of Fort Ragusa was undergoing this operation by blasting, we could perceive some of the men running as usual from where an explosion was to take place; it went off soon after, carrying at the same time a human being up into the air. It was discovered that the unfortunate person was Lieutenant Thiele, a German engineer officer, in our service; he had imprudently gone back to the fatal spot, under the idea that the fuse had gone out, but the melancholy sequel shows that he had been mistaken.

Almaraz being at length rendered incapable of defence, and its bridge of boats annihilated, the men abandoned themselves to joy: the whole of the following night was spent in feasting, drinking, and singing; every remembrance of their fallen comrades being drowned in present enjoyment. Next morning, we marched off, so heavily laden with spoil that, at one time, the colonel threatened to cut off our haversacks, in order to make swifter travellers. After halting in our former encampment in the mountains, we returned to Truxillo; here the, inhabitants received us with great rejoicings, on account of our late successes: by the by, I may mention here, that the Almaraz exploit had (in our own opinion, at least) closed the balance of valour with the heroes of Rodrigo and Badajoz, although on a smaller scale.

To gratify the people and us, at this time of general conviviality, the authorities of Truxillo ordered a bull-fight to be performed in the *Plaça*, or public square., I suspect this fight was conducted on a more humble plan than what is done, on some occasions; no armed horse or foot attacked the bull in this instance, which is the usual manner, according to book accounts; the animal was merely fastened by a long rope to a ring, in the middle of the square; this gave him a good deal, of scope: the Spaniards then ran up and shook cloths or handkerchiefs in his face, till he was rendered furious: that was the time of the cream of the sport, as it seemed, for at the moment the bull was stooping to gore its tormentor, the latter contrived, with admirable agility, to escape, to the infinite delight and edification of the spectators.

From the skill of the Spaniards at such exercises, I believe the entertainment would have passed over without bloodshed, had not one of the British, a 60th rifleman foolishly mixed among the combatants; but, of course, being far inferior to them in adroitness, he was overtaken by the ferocious beast, and tossed with dreadful violence into the air: the hapless man was taken up in a shocking condition; he expired soon after.

We continued our march to Merida, where a prisoner, the French governor of Almaraz, died of his wounds; he was buried with every military honour due to his rank. Leaving this place, we arrived at Almandralego ere a new chaplain was appointed to preach to the brigade; instead of laying his books only on the drum-head, he suddenly jumped himself, with all the agility of a mountebank, on the top of that noisy instrument; this action naturally drew a deafening laugh from the soldiery, they expecting every instant to see the chaplain make his exit through the skin: he had almost commenced an oration, when Colonel Stewart, of the 50th, warned him of the mistake,

Our army now received orders to make a diversion in the south, while Wellington was moving northward to Salamanca, leaving Almandralego, therefore. We marched for some time, passing through the towns of Zafra and Llerana: the enemy's flying parties, who infested Estremadura, were driven before us in all directions, our advanced parties of cavalry being engaged every day with them: we halted, at length on the outskirts of Balranga, on account of doubts existing that the enemy were in that place.

In the course of the night, the whole camp was thrown into an uproar, a crashing and tumbling of the piled arms were heard, accompanied by a furious rushing sound: the idea that the French cavalry had broken in upon us was taken for granted; but the alarm was instantaneously quashed, by a discovery that the cause of it arose from one poor, stray bullock, which had probably escaped from the knife of the butcher. Next day we marched into the town, where we took up our quarters. Provisions had not been abundant of late; the sight of a large flock of sheep, therefore, awakened every appetite; but how to get at them was the question: no reasonable pretext for so doing being at hand, some bright genius or other raised a cry that they were "*French sheep.*"

This was enough; for with one accord, the whole brigade rushed upon the flock, and seized every one of them, the poor Spanish shepherds standing all the while mute with astonishment at such a wanton act of superior power. I know not whether these men were remunerated for their loss or not: at any rate, we were more successful in this exploit than Don Quixote was in his memorable attack of the fleecy warriors.

Balranga, the utmost limit of our southern excursions, is situated, on the confines, of Andalusia, about twenty leagues from

Cadiz, and not far from the Mediterranean: the celebrated range of mountains called Sierra Morena is close by the town. This Sierra is, I believe, the supposed scene of some of Don Quixote's pranks. Wheeling about, we returned to Zafra.

During our stay at this place a bull-fight took place, which a second time proved disastrous to my countrymen. Just as some pickets were going from the town to the camp, the bull appeared on its way to the *Plaça*; some Spaniards led him along with a rope, but no sooner did he observe our men, than a furious charge was made upon them; they not being prepared to encounter such an uncouth foe, prudently took refuge in the surrounding houses and stairs: one unfortunate man, however, was ripped up along the whole back, by a single blow, just at the moment he was stooping to enter a door.

The grisly savage then continued his course up a street, where the band was playing before Colonel Cadogan's door, seated at the same time round a large table: the musicians, being well aware of their inferiority to Orpheus, in point of ability to tame brutes, also fled in every direction; the beast now employed himself in smashing the table and overturning the forms; in this havoc, the music-books were all torn and scattered about, neither did the band-master's costly clarinet escape the general destruction.

At length, the sentinel at the colonel's door took courage, and made a thrust at the bull with a fixed bayonet, which merely glanced off his thick scull, without doing much damage, although the bayonet was bent: this attack served, however, to startle him, and he set off at full speed towards a narrow street, where the regimental guard was loitering about: some of the men escaped into the guard-house, others got behind a bullock-car; but one foolhardy Irishman stood rooted to the spot, in spite of his comrades' entreaties to save himself.

This man had been at all times of a cross and perverse disposition, doing everything in the true spirit of contradiction: unhappily, he supported his character in this instance, and thereby drew upon himself the punishment of vain temerity: the bull coming up, mangled him in a dreadful manner; this and the former victim died in great agony.

The conductors of the bull had kept hold of the rope the whole time; but finding it impossible to restrain his impetuosity, they still held on, and ran as he ran: he was at length forced into the *Plaça*, and the fight took place, notwithstanding the recent tragical events.

From Zafra we marched to Villa Franca; it was about this time that the news of Wellington's signal victory of Salamanca reached us: liquor was served out; and the colonel acted as fugleman again, in consequence of the joyful event. The 50th regiment having all been seized with sore eyes, they were sent to a village in the neighbouring mountains, for the benefit of better air, and to prevent the rest of the brigade from being infected; this circumstance made our duty harder than usual, until the invalids recovered. We now set off to Don Bonito, and reached it after a circuitous march of five days.

In these marches through Estremadura, the weather was insufferably hot: scarcely a breath of air was stirring, and the long drought had formed such quantities of dust on the roads, that the tread of so many feet raised it about us in clouds, making every one like a miller with the whiteness. When the smallest symptoms of a passing breeze appeared, every tongue was hung out, for the purpose of obtaining a momentary refreshing coolness.

Sometimes a good deal of misery was avoided by travelling at night: on such occasions we went along very pleasantly, a number of the men singing their best songs, others joining in the choruses. While lying encamped after a long march, it was surprising to see with what vivacity the men started up to pursue the hares, which sometimes unwarily entered the camp; never did one escape when the whole brigade joined in the chace, uttering loud yells—the noise striking it powerless with terror.

It being the fruit season at our present residence, Don Bonito, many nocturnal parties were formed by the men, for the purpose of secretly pillaging the neighbouring gardens: immense loads of fruit (chiefly figs) were brought in upon spread greatcoats; shirts, formed into temporary bags, were also used for the same laudable purpose. An old Spaniard made a remark, that the French had reaped his harvest last year—we had done it this—but that he would have it to himself next year. This random prophecy proved eventually true, as the belligerent powers did not make this part of the country the theatre of war again.

CHAPTER 7

Death of Cadogan

Lord Wellington's army having entered Madrid after the Battle of Salamanca, we set off in the direction of the metropolis, as I presumed for the purpose of co-operating with them. We crossed the Guadiana, and traversed our old road again, passing through Truxillo to Almaraz. At the latter place, some of the men went down to the ruins of Fort Napoleon, to examine the scene of their former exploit. They found several of our men's bodies, which had been but partially covered with earth: the rain had washed it off, and exposed the grinning skeletons to view: even in this state, a well-known sergeant was discovered amongst them, by a particular mark on his coat. The visitors took care to hide them better from the air, and came away affected with the gloomy silence of the place, which had been so very different only a few months before.

Crossing the Tagus here on pontoons, we marched to Talavera: here I went, according to my usual custom, to look for the house I had lodged in the first time we were in the country; but, after a long search, I found the whole street where it had been situated was reduced to a heap of ruins—such a woeful change had four years of this cursed war produced. Leaving this dilapidated town, we pursued our way through a beautiful country: ripe grapes hung temptingly within our reach on both sides of the road; every finger was stretched to have a pull at them; but Colonel Cadogan keeping a strict lookout for the benefit of the unfortunate proprietors, little could be obtained in daylight, although this abstinence was abundantly made up for at night.

It is difficult to restrain men in such cases: the work of a few is nothing in comparison; but the labour of our multitudes was sufficient to destroy a whole vintage;—anyone that was detected in the act was punished, by being obliged to carry the bass-drum for a certain distance.

At length we approached the famous city of Toledo, and were welcomed everywhere with joyful acclamations: a number of nuns turned out of a convent, shaking handkerchiefs and shouting many *vivas* to us, while we were marching by; the town bells were set a-ringing, and an illumination ordered to be prepared, to celebrate our arrival. Such unequivocal demonstrations of real joy arose from the cheerful aspect of Spanish affairs at that time; the capital being recovered, and the whole kingdom nearly rescued from French thraldom.

I walked through the town to view the illuminations, which, upon the whole, was much like what is seen in our own country, with the exception of a tall spire, which was hung from top to bottom with variegated lamps: this certainly had a very brilliant effect. We left this interesting scene, and advanced to Aranjuez—a place remarkable for containing a splendid palace belonging to the Spanish royal family, situated amidst rich gardens, extensive parks, and noble avenues of trees, the River Tagus running through the centre of the grounds: but the description of such enchanting scenery must be left to the pens of a Scott or a Radcliffe; I own my incompetency to the task with the utmost humility. During our stay here, many of our officers visited Madrid, to enjoy the festivities which had been going on there ever since the entrance of the British.

From Aranjuez we moved to Ponte Duino, farther up the Tagus. One day, while a number of men were bathing in the river, a party of French cavalry came in sight. This naturally caused everyone to make the best of his way towards the shore, with the exception of a droll fellow, who stood for some time slapping a nameless part in derision of the Frenchmen. On seeing this, some of them unloosed their carbines and fired a shot or two at our hero, who then thought proper to fly. Some of the

60th Riflemen turned out from their quarters on hearing the noise; and by discharging a few shot, soon made the horsemen scamper out of sight.

At Ponte Duino I first had an opportunity of witnessing the mode of feeding among the Spanish soldiery: in this respect it must be granted that they were much more military than ourselves;—for example, I saw a party of them drawn up an the form of a circle, with a kettle of soup in the centre; one man at a time advanced to the object of attack, and after having swallowed a single spoonful of the mess, he returned to his place and resumed a stiff, erect posture; the next did the same, and so on in rotation till the whole of the soup disappeared.

Suddenly we were aroused by the near approach of 70,000 French, consisting of the armies of Soult and Suchet, from Andalusia and Valencia: their late reverses in the north had caused this hostile movement. Every idea of stopping the progress of such a formidable host being given up, we left our present station at night-fall, for the purpose of joining Wellington, who had now relinquished the siege of Burgos.

We continued to push on with little intermission till the following night, when, as we were trudging along a bridge, very tired, and half asleep, a sort of panic arose; some fixing their bayonets, others jumping upon the parapet walls, either to see or escape the expected danger. However, as nothing appeared, we quietly encamped, laughing at the false alarm, which, after all, had arisen from one of the men thinking he had seen a horse fly by him like a flash of lightning!

Previous to marching again, we were ordered to empty our haversacks of a quantity of potatoes, which had come into our possession—no matter how. Leaving many piled heaps of these roots on the ground, we journeyed for two days, and arrived at Madrid, not in it—for a short halt only was made at the end of a bridge, until the British garrison marched out of the city and joined us. We then moved off altogether, abandoning the capital to the enemy. Thus, although it was the second time, I had been close to Madrid, yet fate seemed to have decreed that I should never enter it: no great matter, some will say; perhaps so.

The Escurial was the end of our next stage: alterations had taken place here, too, since my first, visit. A strong wall was built across, the principal street, filled with loopholes. This work had been projected by Joseph Buonaparte, to defend himself from the Guerillas, who had extended their incursions to the palace gates. It will, perhaps, serve to give an idea of the unwieldy size of this mighty structure, the palace—to say what was actually done; to wit, that our whole division of 20,000 men lay for a night in its lobbies or passages. The rooms were locked up, and the priests had fled to some more congenial soil, as we supposed.

From the Escurial we crossed the same pass in the mountains which we had crossed four years before; and passing afterwards through Alva de Tormas, the main body of Wellington's army joined us. Nigh to the latter place, immense heaps of human and horse bones lay whitening in the air: the owners of them had been slain in the pursuit, after the Battle of Salamanca. The enemy having now concentrated the whole of their forces in Spain, for the avowed purpose of driving the British back to Portugal again, Lord Wellington still continued encamped in the vicinity of Alva de Tormas, but detached our brigade into that town, to defend it as long as possible. We found the walls of the place old and dilapidated: however, preparations for a vigorous resistance were made—300 men were posted in an old castle, and the streets barricaded with loose stone dikes.

Next day the French Army appeared, advancing directly upon the town we commenced skirmishing with their advanced parties; but orders being given to refrain from acting on the offensive, we lay close behind the entrenchments, such as they were. Meanwhile the enemy opened up a heavy fire from twenty pieces of cannon, which, by our precautions for personal safety, only wrought destruction among the deserted houses: a man at my side had a narrow escape—he saw a cannon-ball coming towards him, but had the presence of mind to draw back; while doing so, the ball grazed his forehead, carried of some skin, and only rendered the place of a blackish red colour: Colonel Cadogan soon afterwards saw the man, and remarked that he must have had a d——d hard skull.

The enemy continued to batter away the whole day without intermission, or receiving a single answering shot from us, we being only ready to repel in case of their coming to close quarters. While in this situation, one of the men having picked up some unknown sort of root, and eat of it, along with another man, they both became stupefied, and even furious, striking every person near them, and playing the most antic tricks; upon which an officer, under the idea that they were drunk, ordered them to be confined: this was effected with no small difficulty, a stout resistance of kicking and sprawling being made on their part.

On the following morning, orders came from Wellington that we should abandon the post, the enemy having crossed the river unperceived the preceding evening; and they would have probably surrounded us had we not retired, leaving 300 Spaniards in the castle: after blowing up a bridge in the course of the retreat, we joined the grand army in safety. It was afterwards reported, that these Spaniards had held their station courageously for seven days before surrendering.

The whole army now moved off, taking its way by a road leading through an immense forest: a pretty long march brought us to its edge. We then found ourselves on the field of Salamanca, where we formed immediately on the ridge which had been the position of the French on that bloody occasion. The ground everywhere betrayed symptoms of the late death-game, by the legs and arms which stuck out in full view: these were also convincing proofs of the manifold toils of the military sextons.

Our ruminations, were soon cut short by the enemy emerging from the wood—instantly, therefore, a company of the 60th rifle corps were detached to skirmish with them; but scarcely had they left us, when a body of French cavalry were seen advancing at a gallop for the purpose of charging—they perhaps would have made short work with the riflemen, if our artillerymen had not, by a well-timed discharge, compelled them to wheel round and return as quick as they came. I observed one fellow in particular: he was lifted up from his saddle by a cannonball, and fell to the ground seemingly unhurt; for the next instant he rose and ran off: his horse also took to flight, but in a different direction.

The cannon being placed in a position admirably adapted for committing mischief, they were opened upon the enemy's columns with terrible effect: at every discharge, a space was seen in their ranks which would admit a waggon! Lord Wellington and his staff remained for some time stationary in front of our regiment: as several of them had telescopes, a more particular estimation of the enemy's loss could thus be obtained, at almost every shot. Someone of those spectators who had glasses encouraged the artillery, by crying out—"That is a good one!"

The enemy at length sheltered themselves in the wood, thinking, probably, that affairs were taking a too tragical turn: an *aide-de-camp*, in my hearing, said that their loss could not be less than 1,000—this is a round number, to be sure, but in my opinion not far from the truth. Strange it is, however, that the minds of men have been so perverted as to exult according to the number of their slain opponents!

We entered the wood while it was getting dark, and were obliged to stretch ourselves on the ground supperless—water, that requisite for cooking, not being at hand. Next morning the whole army formed upon the same ground as before: the French Army was also drawn up in formidable array. Every appearance of a bloody battle was in prospect; but on the enemy's attempting to turn our right. Lord Wellington gave the order to retreat in the direction of Portugal. Thus had the Spanish campaign come to nought again.

Our regiment was left by itself on a height, for the purpose of amusing the enemy while the British Army was filing off. We stood a full hour shivering in a storm of rain, till the last of them had passed by, when a general officer rode back from the rear, and cried to Cadogan—"If you do not move from that station, your men will be prisoners in less than ten minutes." We waited not for a second invitation, but set off through some ploughed, fields, which, as usual, clogged our feet—the heavy rain still continuing, and reducing the earth to a pulp.

For a further precaution against the pursuers, we formed a square: one of the companies performing its part awkwardly in this evolution, the colonel threatened to leave the men behind to the enemy: such a menace was perhaps less terrific than he imagined. By the time we reached the road, the rain had increased to such a degree that the water was up to our knees: in the midst of this interesting scene, a number of soldiers' wives and children, mounted on asses, finding it impossible to keep up with us, began a concert, of cries and tears; but as no assistance could be afforded, they fell into the enemy's hands.

All the while, our cavalry and the enemy's kept firing at each other—being muffled up in cloaks, they loaded their carbines under these coverings in perfect security from the rain: the skirmishing would have had a very picturesque appearance to an unconcerned spectator. We were nearly out of breath when a junction was effected with the rest of the brigade—a very hasty trot having been resorted to latterly. Colonel Stewart called to Cadogan, that he had never expected to see us again. I believe, in this instance, we kept the old precept well in mind; to wit, "a good pair of heels is worth two pair of hands."

That evening, bivouacking again in the woods, we were startled by the noise of musquetry in several directions: after all, it turned out that an immense drove of hogs had occasioned this alarm; they had probably been placed in the forest for the sake of security; but that they no longer found, few escaping from the ball and the bayonet. This unexpected supply created a redundancy of food, and every belly and haversack was filled. Next night, while reposing our limbs, and cooking, after a long day's march, a large body of French cavalry was observed advancing towards us: this was particularly provoking, we being obliged to empty our kettles and stand to arms: some cannon were brought to the edge of the wood, and preparations made to allow our cavalry to act at a fit opportunity.

The enemy having approached to the desired distance, the artillery gave them a warm salute, and a company of the 28th, who were rearguard, gave them also a volley; our cavalry then rushed out, charged, and put the Frenchmen to flight, after wounding and making several of them prisoners. One of our horsemen led in a prisoner who had received a deep gash on the cheek: this fellow was so enraged with his conductor, that he poured forth torrents of abuse and oaths, such as "*sacre Dieu!*" &c,. but the Englishman returned an answer for every imprecation, by giving him a thump across the back with the flat side of his sabre.

This "brush" having removed us to a marshy part of the forest, we were obliged, for our own comfort, to cut down branches to sleep upon for the remainder of the night. An hour before daylight the army moved off, the 71st acting as a rearguard for the coming day: by dawn, our old friends, the French cavalry, could be seen indistinctly through a heavy mist, which still lay on the ground: two men were sent out to ascertain the reality of their approach.

Before the scouts had proceeded a dozen of yards, they were fired upon: this was enough. We immediately formed square and stood for some time, then moved on in the same attitude, leaving several drowsy stragglers behind. The French were still following with unwearied assiduity, although always kept well at bay by our gallant dragoons.

Still traversing this tiresome wood, we halted after crossing a river: a heavy firing was heard about this time, the enemy having assaulted the rear of Wellington's army, but without any material success. Our bivouac this evening would have been no way unworthy of furnishing a subject for a painter.—Figure to yourself, reader, a large body of men sitting on the ground amidst water, at least six inches deep, with rain descending upon them by bucketsful; fires, where any could be kept alive, sending forth volumes of smoke, and, at chance times, a transient gleam of flame, which only served to illume for an instant our ragged raiment, stained haversacks, long beards, and way-worn countenances.

Next morning, we marched with alacrity from our "lodgings on the cold ground," leaving several men unable to move, in consequence of cramp in the stomach. The road wound through the centre of lofty mountains, down the sides of which brooks, converted into torrents by the constant rain, fell with if brawling noise, making at the same time numerous streams across the road, every one of which we had to ford, often up to the middle.

We halted that night in security, our retreat being terminated; the enemy, having given up the pursuit, chiefly, it is supposed, on account of our arrival in the vicinity of Ciudad Rodrigo. This was certainly a well-conducted and fortunate retreat: undoubtedly, no small loss add misery were experienced in it; yet how light in comparison were they to those of Corunna!

Parting from Wellington's army again, we marched to a village, which was universally denominated the "smoky town" by the men, a continual smoke hanging over its crooked streets; yet scarcely so deleterious, I believe, as the pestilential vapours of the Glasgow and Manchester public works. Removing to the town of Coria, we received some arrears of pay, which were immediately squandered away upon wine; the kettles of that fascinating liquor never standing empty as long as the means of supplying them lasted.

Our prodigality elicited a remark from a Spanish landlady which would have done no discredit to any "thrifty auld Scotch wife,"—she expressing her surprise that we spent so much money in wine, and never thought of buying shirts to our backs: in fact, it must be owned, that we were as ill, if not worse off, in this respect, than Falstaff's famous crew—they possessed a shirt and a half, but we could not boast of one at that time!

From Coria we removed to Monte Moso, the most advanced post in the direction of the enemy's cantonments; here another draft joined us: it was in this manner that all-devouring Death required to be fed. New-Year's-Day, 1813, was spent with due honour, by carousing in the usual manner,—the favourite song was the "Banks of the River Clyde:" the allusion to home explains the cause of this,—for, of course, the uppermost wish of many was the desire soon to reach that haven, although such a prospect had not the remotest appearance of being realised, at least at that period: for my part, I almost wish, at the present moment, that Spain contained me still.

We next took up our quarters in Igal, a village situated near Placentia; our lodgings were more comfortable now, two of us only being billeted upon each inhabitant. One day, talking with the landlady of our house, she was asked, why she did not send her daughters to a nunnery? she replied—"Send them to be *putias!!*" *viz.* courtesans. It would be foolish and illiberal to take this solitary instance as the voice of the whole nation; but from other circumstances known to us, she was not far wrong in her opinion of these seminaries of pretended religion.

About this time, the French had the boldness to send in a demand for a contribution from the people of Boho, a village at no great distance from us: the 50th were instantly despatched to occupy that place—which was as much as to say—"take it if you dare." Quitting Igal, we shifted our lodgings to Puerto Banios, in the time of Lent; which, although it did not in any way interfere with our cooking operations, yet there is little doubt it would disturb those of the inhabitants. Lent seemed also to give rise to many processions and other Catholic ceremonies: I observed, in particular, a troop of boys, who were busily employed making insufferable noises with large clappers, to rejoice at the signal victory obtained by Michael over the devil, as I was told. Why should the superstitions of ancient Greece and Rome be laughed at? They yield not in absurdity to the story I have mentioned.

While we lay in Puerto Banios, a troop of wolves entered the village, and devoured a hog and a bullock; the neighbourhood was also so much infested by the wolves, that the *alcalde* gave rewards for bringing in their heads. It would appear that this had stimulated the Spaniards much, every door in the place being graced with the desired trophy. One morning, the rolling of musquetry was heard in the direction of Boho: we immediately set off, full speed, to lend the 50th any assistance that might be required, but on our arrival at their quarters, it was discovered that the French had paid them a visit betimes, and had happily been beaten off. Soon after this the 50th and we changed places, we removing to Boho.

At that delightful place I got into exceedingly good quarters, being lodged in the house of a rich man, or at least a proprietor of several houses. I may say with safety, that from the day of leaving home I had never found real comfort until the hospitable Don Alphonso received me into his dwelling. His family only consisting of himself, wife, and daughter (a girl of thirteen), I, along with my comrade, dined with them every day—they cooking our rations. The excessive kindness of these benevolent people was the more acceptable to us after such a life of toil and misery. So solicitous were they for our welfare, that if we at any time happened to be later than usual in coming home, the landlord himself, would search through the whole village for the purpose of bringing us to the house.

Our stay in Boho rendered the place what is called "extremely gay," the young women and our men getting very gracious: dancing formed an important part of the amusements. Even on Sundays the girls would come out into the streets, playing on *panderas*; dances were then struck up, which many of the men joined in; others, more scrupulous, refrained on account of the day.

Summer approaching apace, active preparations began to be made for taking the field again: tents were served out, three to each company; kettles were also distributed, portable enough to be carried on the back. This was a wise regulation, we being enabled to commence cooking the moment a march ended; whereas, formerly, the kettles were of such an unwieldy construction, that they were obliged to be placed upon mules, which, by their tardy gait, were always far behind, and thereby kept us from our meals for many a grievous hour.

Our regiment was reviewed here by General Stewart, who, about the same time, performed an action for which we ever after held him in the highest respect. Seeing how much sentinels felt when bearing about a heavy knapsack, especially when exposed to the rays of a burning sun, he ordered that henceforth they should be at liberty to lay the knapsacks on the ground while on duty; saying, also, that there was always plenty of time to lift them, if any alarm should take place.

On the 21st of May we bid *adieu* to repose and the good people of Boho, multitudes of whom turned out to convoy us. Aged parents were seen running distractedly about, endeavouring to drag, back their weeping daughters: every man, of us, had placed a handkerchief on his ramrod, as a kind of farewell signal. Notwithstanding the remonstrances of the old folks, and Col. Cadogan himself, thirty young women obstinately persisted in attaching themselves to as many of our men.

The colonel was unwilling to use force in getting rid of the women; but he hit upon an effectual method for doing so gradually—this was by allowing them no rations. The paramours bore awhile with this regulation, through means of sharing; but times of scarcity coming on afterwards, a coolness took place on both sides, as might be expected; and the damsels dropt off by degrees, takings up with muleteers, or anyone who could afford to feed them.

Having encamped for a few days in the vicinity of Boho, for the purpose of joining the other portions of the army that were assembling from the various cantonments, myself and comrade took advantage of the interim to visit our benefactor Alphonso. The worthy family received us with unaffected joy: we were invited to dinner; and many a pressing invitation was given to me to return after *la guerre,* and make their house my home. I wish to God I had done so—irrevocable circumstances prevent me now: besides, who knows if they are in the land o' the living?

But to return to the subject—several Spanish soldiers had been quartered in the house since our departure; they, seeing us so well treated, could scarce conceal their rage and envy; and all the time of the visit regarded us with very sinister looks: but the actions of such fellows were beneath contempt. The parting moment came at length: we took leave of Alphonso, the amiable Esperanza, and her mother, forever, and returned with sorrowful hearts to the camp. Some may think it childish that I should mention that these almost strangers have been the leading characters in the drama of my dreams; and on these occasions they have seemed always to be near me, as I thought, while I never could obtain an opportunity of speaking to them.

But realities must be resumed;—it was not difficult to perceive that the efforts of the enemy had begun to slacken; and that their locust-like hosts descended seldomer into the peninsula: the obvious cause of this arose, as it is well known, from the vast Russian expedition, which cramped every other operation.

We began our march northward, on account of the French abandoning the south of Spain without compulsion—unless a decrease of numbers and supplies can be called so. The weather being exceedingly sultry at the first outset, one of the stoutest men in our company was so much affected by it as to fall suddenly to the ground in the throes of death, grasping at every object around him, and being quite insensible: he was placed in a waggon, where death ended his cares. We all ascribed this man's misfortune to a habit he had of wearing his cap too far off his forehead, and thought he must have undoubtedly been sunstruck.

After passing Salamanca, we were joined by the Oxford Blues and the King's Life Guards, from England: their finery, me thought, should have saved them from the tarnishing effects of the peninsular war. Tedious marches by day, and encamping at night, brought the whole army safe to the environs of Vittoria; the enemy had also concentrated their forces within three leagues of that place.

Some desultory warfare had taken place; but it was not till the 21st of June that Vittoria was numbered among our victories. On the morning of that day we halted, after passing through Puebla, and made preparations for battle: the cavalry and horse artillery being ranged along the front of the infantry, the march was then continued. While thus advancing, one of our Irishmen expressed his apprehension that the 71st would not have an opportunity of distinguishing themselves, and that there would be "no mention of us in the newspapers." Poor fellow, little did he know how soon we were destined to suffer more loss than any of the other regiments, and that his own death-wound was to be received in the fray.

Lord Wellington having contemplated the seizure of the heights of Puebla, where the left of the enemy's army was posted, the obvious executors of the project were the right of our army, which was as usual composed of Hill's division. It was not long before, orders came to open out right and left, and for the 71st to advance. "Come on, my lads," said Cadogan; "come on, and get hairy knapsacks." We accordingly moved forward through the opening made for us, and soon had an unobstructed view of the whole French Army, drawn up in lines: turning then to the right, we began the ascent of the heights.

To have thus obtained the honour; as it were, of "opening the ball," some may think ought to have made us what is called "burn with enthusiasm;" but I could perceive no such feeling, nor even common satisfaction: the only words uttered were invectives and murmurs at the steepness of the heights, and the slippery state of the grass. I knew that another regiment placed in our situation would have been an object of envy; but the fact is, fighting had begun to lose its novelty.

When the summit of the heights was reached, we found ourselves close to the enemy: a line was then instantly formed, and a volley fired, followed by three cheers. The enemy returned the fire, but soon began to retrograde; upon which we pressed on It was at this important moment that the gallant Cadogan fell, as he rode along the front of the regiment. While in the very act of turning round to cheer us on, the fatal bullet had struck him between the haunch buttons: feeling the wound mortal, he desired himself to be carried to an eminence, where, a full view of the engagement might be obtained: this request was of course complied with.

Meanwhile, the command devolved upon Major Cother, who still led us forward for some distance: liberty to halt was then given. One of the men succeeded in abstracting a loaf from the knapsack of a slain Frenchman: the generous finder coming to satisfy his own appetite, immediately distributed his treasure through the whole company: each had only a morsel,—but keen hunger rendered such a gift sweeter than honey.

A body of Spaniards, under the command of Murillo (the, Tyrant of South America), now marched by us to attack the enemy; soon afterwards we also moved on, three deep, along the ridge of a hill. Already it was evident that the Spaniards had found their enterprise too hot: many of them were to be seen skulking ignominiously to the rear, under various pretexts: some pretended a want of ammunition; others showed an affected solicitude for wounded men, by attending them, carefully to a place of safety: four or five men scrupled not thus to leave the field with a single wounded one, but the idea of returning never once entered their heads!

A strong body of French, posted on a rising ground, began to impede our march by a destructive fire: almost every moment a man fell, either killed or wounded. Disregarding the heavy loss, however, we succeeded in forming with our right under a rocky cliff, in a position rather higher than that of our opponents, which enabled us to return their fire with interest. It is somewhat remarkable, that for a long time during this sanguinary contest, a party of the enemy should have remained undiscovered, perched on the top of the cliff above us: these were the fellows that securely poured down a perpendicular fire, which had such fatal effects; the balls striking the men's backs, and going through their heads and ears: such wounds would have appeared disgraceful in any other case but this.

Major Cother received a wound; and I *myself* had the trouble of picking a bullet out of my trowsers, where it had lodged in the most complaisant manner, without even grazing the skin: another leaden almond contrived to break the swivel of my musquet!

The party, who may be said to have been preying on our vitals, were at length disclosed to view, and answered with firing as well as our circumstances could allow: without doubt, they had hitherto found their safety in the noise, smoke, and confusion, occasioned, by the unabated raging of our engagement with the main body. Meanwhile, the enemy in the plains, desirous

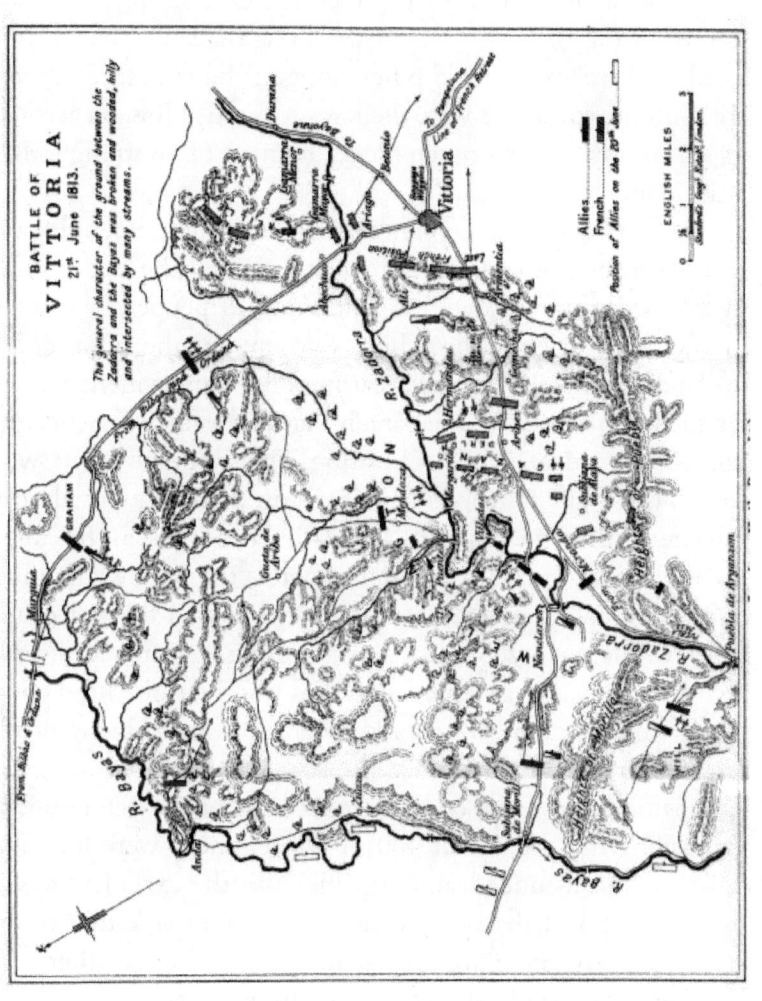

of regaining the important heights which we had wrested from them, detached a column of 5,000 men, led, it is said, by both Joseph Buonaparte and Jourdan: with this force they advanced to the assistance of their comrades, sounding their military music at the same time with great pomp. Our strong Italian no sooner heard, the approach of the new assailants, than, saying hastily, "I be damme if I stop here longer;" he ran off to the rear with infinite speed: we were the less surprised at this, on account of our having always a much higher opinion of his strength than of his courage.

The enemy's reinforcement now came in sight, ascending the eminences beneath us. We immediately seized the opportunity such a situation afforded, by continuing to pepper them with murderous efficiency the whole way up; but the imprudence of standing the onset of such fearful odds being evident, we descended into a hollow, and scarcely was this well done, when the French formed on our old position. The 50th and 92nd, who had all the while remained in reserve, no sooner saw us clear of the enemy, than they opened a well-timed, but distant fire upon them: this was to favour our retreat across the hollow: the musquetry ceased, however, the moment we joined the rest of the brigade. The enemy, awed by our imposing appearance, did not venture to advance a step further: thus was their intention completely thwarted, the conquered heights of Puebla being firmly retained in our possession.

It is time, however, to look at the cost of the achievement. On calling the roll, about 400 of the regiment were found to be killed and wounded, among which was the exact half of our company; and of the sixteen men who bore the kettles of the company, only three were present; it would appear, therefore, that the cooks had been particularly unfortunate.

The rest of the army, extending from our regiment to the extreme left, had, during the course of the day, obtained some splendid advantages; so much so, that about dusk a general and rapid retreat commenced along the whole of the enemy's line; upon which, every part of our army pursued with hasty strides.

Our feelings were destined to experience a severe trial, in passing over the identical ground where our slaughtered comrades lay. As soon as the wounded were aware of our presence, they set up faint cries for water, to assuage the burning thirst which is the inevitable attendant of blood-gushing wounds; they even invoked our assistance by name.

A young man, well known to me, implored my aid with the most piteous language; I had only time to ask in what place of the body he was wounded; the reply was, "in the back," by which I knew that it was mortal. Another man, a sergeant, we saw in a sitting posture, with both of his eyes turned out on the cheeks, a ball having entered the side of his forehead: he too was calling for water. Duty—inexorable duty—compelled us to shut our ears to the horrible distress, and pass on as indifferently as if so many sheep bled in a slaughter-house.

Darkness caused a halt: the excessive fatigues of the day rendered this repose doubly acceptable. On examining my shoulder, I found it of an ebony colour, in consequence of the numerous rebounds of the musquet.

The Battle of Vittoria having terminated this evening, it is necessary to say something regarding it; but this something is only from hearsay, as might be expected. The aggregate number of the Allied Army was superior to that of the French: the loss on each side was about equal. We made few prisoners; but this was abundantly made up by the capture of their immense train of artillery, and all the rest of their military luggage; besides which, the victory enabled us to reach the frontiers of France, without suffering much molestation.

By the by, an officer and twelve men had been sent to bury the body of the lamented Cadogan, who had died on the hill, and had been carried from thence to the grave across a horse. The situation of that grave is only known to the interring parties, they having dug it hastily in the most convenient field that could be found. One would have thought that Cadogan's death should have created a greater sensation than it actually did; but when it is considered how uncertain and miserable our own lives were, our apathy will cease to be wondered at.

Next morning, while we were busily engaged in baking and boiling a little flour, which we had received the preceding evening, the word was given to fall into the line of march. Our regiment either did not hear the command, or was not willing to hear it: this negligence caused our major's wrath to be kindled against us. He came up to the lines and rode furiously along through the fires, overturning kettles, and committing a terrible devastation amongst the cooking apparatus.

Having thus roused us to a sense of duty, by the assistance of his horse's hoofs, we moved on gloomily enough—not so much on account of the loss of our breakfast as of our friends; the late dreadful gap in the regiment having become more observable than before, on account of many marching side by side with strangers, instead of well-known comrades; in fact, we scarcely knew our places in the ranks.

Passing by the town of Vittoria without halting, we began to observe that the road was strewed with innumerable written papers and regimental books: these were certainly new features in the wreck of a flying army. Halting at night, amidst heavy rain, a new system of bivouacking was adopted: parties of three men sitting down on their knapsacks, close to each other, and a blanket being then wrapped round the trio, served to ward off the storm in some degree. The rain continued, without intermission, all the following day, accompanied by thunder and lightning. An officer and his horse fell victims to the fiery fluid. We contrived, however, to reach the environs of Pampeluna, in spite of the muddy roads and raging elements.

The strong fortress of Pampeluna being still in the possession of the enemy, we encamped before it, in expectation of having some hot work at a siege. The garrison were to be distinctly seen, loitering, about, and leaning over the walls, surveying us with great *sangfroid*, but instead of the British, an army of Spaniards was intrusted with the siege. Leaving the camp, therefore, we moved on towards the Pyrenees.

Chapter 8

Brutal Inhumanity

From the extreme length of the lofty barriers of France and Spain—to wit, the Pyrenees—it was judged proper for the allied army to divide into several parties, for the purpose of forming a chain of posts from a certain point to the edge of the Atlantic. One of these parties commenced the Siege of St. Sebastian, a fortress situated at the western extremity of the chain; while we (Hill's army); on the right, advanced upon the valley of Bastan, to which three divisions of the French Army had retired after the Battle of Vittoria. These were, I believe; the only troops the enemy had remaining in the open field throughout the Peninsula.

Having reached the valley on the 4th of July, the same words of command were given as formerly, "Open out right and left, and let the 71st advance:" at this we certainly sprung forward with great alacrity, and scrambled up a mountain's side to turn the enemy. The 50th and 92nd had advanced at the same time, but along the main road.

They contrary to every expectation, were engaged first, and even lost a good number of men; and had not darkness put an end to the affair altogether, we should have been assuredly participators in it. Next day, the army ascended another step of the great Pyrenean stair, the enemy retreating before us; we reached Alisore, where we enjoyed two days of repose. On the 7th, two brigades were detached to drive the enemy further up the hills; the rest of the, division kept advancing along the main road till dusk, when all of us halted, and bivouacked in a brushwood which fringed the brow of a mountain: strict orders to keep silent were given, and no fires were allowed to be lighted.

So close were we to the enemy, that their talking could be distinctly heard. On rising at daylight, a dense cloud or mist was still lazily resting around us, and even far below our situation: the altitude of our position explains this. A faint skirmishing soon commenced, but still the French edged, off, and eventually disappeared.

At length every difficulty was surmounted by our reaching and crowning the summit of the heights of Mayo; and every earthly care was banished for a while by the glorious view which, burst on our eyes: the kingdom of France lay extended before us in all its fertile beauty. The arms were quickly piled and everyone abandoned himself to a variety of reflections. Five years of incessant toil had cleared the Peninsula of Frenchmen and brought us to the borders of their country; but how meagre were these advantages when the vastness of the cost was considered! How much blood had been spilt, and how many taxes had been exacted to gain that empty honour!

The Portuguese soldiers were already gazing on the French territory with savage looks, and planning horrible revenge for the manifold cruelties which had been inflicted upon their country; but, happily for the innocent people; proper steps were taken when we entered France to prevent their suffering for the crimes of brutal mercenaries.

In the midst of our reveries, the sight of some French troops exercising far below, reminded us forcibly that we had labour yet in store. It was on the 8th of July that our tents were pitched along the heights; from that time to the 25th our employments were various: roads were constructed to drag the cannon easily about, and trenches dug around the tents to conduct the dripping water away; this high atmosphere being extremely moist, from the continual passing and repassing of clouds.

The floating suspicion of the French being less "cowed" than was imagined by their late reverses, was fully realised on the 25th, when, by the firing of a signal gun, intimation of their approach was given. Everyone flew to arms and a company of ours was posted on a high peak, while the rest of us moved to the right, at which point the enemy, to the number of 30,000, was ascending from France. The 50th and 92nd had already begun the contest when we joined them. The hostile columns were now at no great distance: soon, therefore, we commenced a fire with all the vivacity which freshness inspires; cutting off such numbers of the enemy, that at one time we were almost led to believe they were retreating, from observing so many of their men hobbling to the rear wounded.

But here we reckoned without our host; the enemy continuing to mount progressively, bearing their heavy losses with great bravery; and at length they gained the top of the heights, in spite of all our efforts.

Inferiority of numbers precluding all chance of our withstanding them with success, an immediate retreat took place; but at every rising ground the firing was renewed;—in short, usual expression of, "disputing every inch of ground," might have been applied with exact justice in this instance. The pursuit was so hot at first, that two regiments of the division were cut off from the main body, and would infallibly have been made prisoners, had not they, with admirable presence of mind, descended the mountains precipitately, by an obscure road.

Meanwhile the rest of us had a narrow escape. While passing the head of a road which went down to France, a strong body of the enemy was seen climbing up to join their comrades; a few minutes longer and we should have been fairly enclosed between the two. Reaching our camp ground, the 71st formed on the declivity of a hill for a short time; the rest of our little army, however, slacked not their pace, but abandoned the whole of the camp equipage. I believe with the exception of our own company's, not a single tent was saved. General Stewart at length gave us orders to retire, which we did by marching round the foot of the peak where our company was posted: this small band was soon heard to be pouring down volleys upon the enemy's van, and successfully resisted every attempt to dislodge them, by rolling down immense stones.

The enemy being again close at hand, a general stand was made, and the hottest engagement I ever witnessed commenced; the enemy all the while endeavouring to surround us, their numerical superiority giving them every advantage for such a purpose; but this we evaded, by frequently shifting our position. We were now in a critical situation, the only hope of a safe retreat resting upon the approaching darkness: the appearance of a fresh body of troops, advancing from the west, also contributed to disconcert us—nobody knew what they were; but on General Stewart saying, "Let us stand to the last," everyone was confirmed in the resolution of still fighting on with energy.

Happily, for us, the dreaded foes turned out to be a reinforcement, from Wellington's army, consisting of the 6th regiment and the Brunswick troops. It was rather a strange coincidence, that one of our men should at such a time recognise a brother in the ranks of the 6th, whom he had not seen for many years; the opportunity for mutual congratulations was short, scarcely extending farther than the mere shaking of hands. Nothing could have been more seasonable than the arrival of these regiments: they interposed between us and the enemy at a time when we were nearly overwhelmed, and began a heavy thundering fire: the French, however, were far from being backward in exchanging shots; as a proof of which, the major of the 6th fell, lifeless from his horse at the very moment he had entered the field. The musquetry only slackened in consequence of nightfall and even then, the flashes served some for a marking point; at length, every noise but the groaning of the wounded was hushed, to the great relief of our deafened ears.

The woeful duty, of calling the roll next took place; the casualties were found to be numerous, particularly in our brigade—for example, the 50th had 300 killed and wounded; the 71st, 200; and the 92nd, 360: our loss, though it appeared inferior to the others, was, in fact, as much in proportion, the Vittoria exploit having rendered us much weaker than they were. *My* company was reduced from 48 men to 11; I was, as usual, amongst the latter number, without having anything to complain of personally;

although a bullet-hole through my coat, and the cutting of the buckle-strap of my cartridge-box, spoke in silent but forcible language of the nearness of death, or wounds at least.

At one period in the course of this eventful day, our ammunition ran so short, that three men in each company only could keep up a constant fire, they being supplied from their comrades' boxes: this plan was adopted to amuse the enemy for a while. It was about the same time that a Spanish muleteer was descried on his course up the hills, bringing a supply of ammunition; but no sooner had the man come near enough to the scene of action to witness its horrors; than he instantly wheeled round, his mule and fled.

Some of the men had a hot chase after the poltroon before he was seized: by dint of mere dragging, they succeeded in placing him near the regiment; at that very juncture, the mule fell, wounded, to the ground. This circumstance, as might be supposed, did not contribute in raising the courage of the muleteer, who disentangled himself from the dying mule, and ran off with the swiftness of a roe, leaving us to disburden the cargo in what manner we chose.

Habit is all-powerful:—inured to death and danger by long practice, the muscles of fear never once exerted their influence on our faces in the day of battle; but with an unconcerned spectator, such as the mule-driver, the case is different: war is not his trade, and self-preservation, the natural stimulus of mankind's actions, predominates in his mind. In the heat of the engagement General Stewart having received a slight wound, and no surgeon being at hand, two of our men had the opportunity of rendering him a little service: they dressed the wound so much to the general's satisfaction, that he noted their names in a pocket-book, and afterwards presented one of them with three guineas; the other lived not to receive a reward.

Not choosing to bear the brunt of a second attack, we stole silently away in the dark: such of the wounded as could crawl followed us with difficulty, while those who could not, injured themselves more by useless, yet touching cries, entreating our

71st Regiment Officer and Private

protection. This retrograding march to Spain, so contrary to expectation, threw a gloom over every mind; strong apprehensions were entertained that all our battles would be to fight "o'er again;" not at our own firesides, but in good earnest. Had our pursuers been led by Buonaparte in all his pristine vigour, there is little doubt but that the suspicion would have been realised.

Soon after daybreak we met parties of cavalry going up, charged with the mission of carrying away the wounded to a place of safety: a good number of these unfortunate men were brought down across the horses' backs. Hardly had we encamped, when the appearance of the French caused the whole division to climb the sides of a mountain, where some repose was obtained till the following morning, at which time the descent was continued till night, the old brushwood sheltering us once more. Here some of the men took advantage of the darkness to cut the rum-barrels from the commissary's mules; drinking and carousing, of course, followed; this led to the detection of the more incautious, who were slightly punished.

We still continued our march towards Pampeluna; a heavy firing was heard on the morning of the 30th; in fact, several engagements had taken place of late, the enemy having penetrated into Spain at more than one point. In the afternoon, they appeared, advancing towards us in great, force; upon which; two companies were posted in a wood, when a pealing of musquetry commenced between them and the French. Our whole brigade was soon engaged; notwithstanding this, we were driven backwards to a range of hills, where quiet was at length obtained. Upon this occasion, the Portuguese troops engaged the French, in a hollow, with the greatest bravery, and lost many men.

This continual mountain-warfare harassed us to an inconceivable degree; so much so, indeed, that death itself was eagerly panted for by many; others had serious thoughts of allowing themselves to fall into the enemy's hands. But the state of affairs began thenceforth to change: Soult's bold efforts to chase the allies from the frontiers of his country were now slackening for want of soldiers.

The next morning, we resumed the offensive, attacking the enemy, who had retired under the covert of a brushwood jungle: some smart skirmishing ensued; but this Indian sort of warfare had its disadvantages, several of our men shooting each other, as the intense thickness of the wood deceived their eyes. At length, the enemy were beat out of their shelter; and no more was seen of them till our invasion of France, General Stewart was severely wounded in this affair; yet in this state, while bearing through the camp, he, with his accustomed good-nature, ordered that every man in the division should have an extra allowance of rum.

Ascending the Pyrenees once more, we reached the Heights of Mayo; the scene of our late conflict. After having reposed our weary limbs for some days, we moved through steep mountain-roads to the valley of Roncesvalles. A residence of three months here completely saturated us with stationary service, which it must be understood was of a severe description. The principal events which took place in this interval were, the surrender of St. Sebastian: and of Pampeluna to our arms; or, more properly speaking, to the arms of Sir Thomas Graham's army, and those of the Spanish troops.

Twelve men belonging to our regiment joined us from Pampeluna: they had been prisoners there ever since the Battle of Vittoria. Starvation had reduced, them do skin and bone, the French garrison having been subjected to the greatest straits for provisions before they submitted to the Spanish Army.

Our own transactions in the valley of Roncesvalles were at least multifarious, if devoid of interest. We were engaged in the building of batteries and block-houses, preparing shells to roll down mountains, without adopting the vulgar method of firing them from mortars: these occupations, along with hard duty, filled up our time for a while. The reappearance of General Stewart, who had completely recovered from his wound gladdened every heart: the whole camp rang with the loud and hearty cheers of the soldiery.

The uncommon noise alarmed many of the officers who were for some time ignorant of its causes. Philosophical sneers may be excited by this, and conclusions made, that it was easy to gain popularity among common soldiers, by giving them a little rum, and the liberty of walking for a short time without burdensome knapsacks. But these formed only a small part of Sir William's benevolent actions: besides, it was notorious to everyone, that he never set baits for applause—all proceeded from innate goodness of heart, and not from weak and unworthy motives.

When the weather became sharp, each brigade of the army had week about of occupying the lofty heights of Altobispo. The climate of that peaked desert continued to wax colder and colder as the year advanced: its severity at length arrived to such a height that the artillery horses were obliged to be taken to the valley, being unable to endure the cold longer. About this time, I was sent up; two of the days in particular, were nearly insufferable; wind of the most tremendous violence blew with unwearied fierceness; no tents could be erected, for they would have been torn to ribands; even in attempting to speak, a serious inconvenience was felt, the wind filling the mouth, fires, when any of our men, succeeded in lighting them, were instantly scattered over the precipices. Judge, then, what our *comforts* must have been!

At length. General Stewart, with his customary attention and humane feeling, ordered that only pickets, instead of a whole brigade, were to remain on the heights. Nobody supposed that the French, would have the hardihood to climb the sides of this "howling wilderness" with a hostile intention; but here we laboured under a mistake; they did make an attempt.

Fifteen men of our regiment happened to be on picket that day: instead of flinching from the unequal contest, they displayed such skill and resolution in attacking the enemy, that the latter thought proper to make a precipitate retreat; the haziness of the atmosphere rendering them unconscious of their own vastly superior numbers: the fifteen men were rewarded with medals.

The morning of the day that the snow came on, I was relieved from picket in a strange condition; our greatcoats were frozen, as it were, into shining steel hauberks, lumps of ice hid our eyebrows and whiskers;—the evidence of the eyes alone could convince us of the possession of our torpid limbs. The picket which relieved us (57th men) were still worse off: a heavy fall of snow, commencing, the consequence was, that three of them died, and the rest had to be brought down on mules, inanimate and frostbitten.

The folly of keeping human being on such a place being now, evident, the guarding was discontinued: in fact, a picket of Esquimaux would have been necessary for the service, if our authorities had persisted in retaining, the post. The snow continued gradually to descend lower, even reaching our encampment in the valley: this circumstance soon constrained the whole division to remove to the village of Roncesvalles for shelter. The smallness of this place incommoded us not a little, the men being literally squeezed into every house, to the great annoyance of the poor inhabitants.

One day a party of us were summoned on fatigue, the ostensible purpose of our mission being to drag in the guns of a battery which lay at some distance, deserted on account of the snow. Some bullocks were provided, under the idea that they would tread a good road in the snow, and by that means facilitate the passage of the cannon. Furnishing ourselves all with sticks, we sallied forth, driving the cattle before but it was soon found that they were either too stupid or too headstrong to go abreast; in short, they dispersed several ways, in spite of our efforts, some of them even running nearly out of sight, in the deeper places of the yielding snow.

To every appearance, the probability of having a bullock-hunt was much greater than that of making a road; when General Stewart detached me, along with five others, to a distant block-house, in order to ascertain the condition of three men who had been posted there for some time. Leaving the dragging party, therefore, we set off, following the course of some lines which had been built in a French and Spanish, war, about twenty years before. When the end of them was attained, we used the precaution of breaking our sticks to pieces, and planting them in the snow, at regular intervals, on the whole way to the block-house, which was at length reached.

The three men, however, were nowhere to be seen: it appeared afterwards, that they had evacuated the house, and returned by a different route. Meanwhile, we were rather loath to return at once from the object of our errand: perhaps this commendable state of mind originated, in some degree, from the sight of a large quantity of biscuits and several little sturdy kegs of rum, with which the corner of the block-house was gracefully bedecked.

After a long deliberation, in which the danger of drinking spirits in the intense cold, and the danger of being punished for pilfering them, were fully discussed, it was carried, by unanimous consent, that a little rum would be of service to us: this was enough; and ere long the liquor was gushing into a shoe, for want of a better dish. We had the wisdom to quaff a small quantity only, at the same time feeding plentifully on the biscuits, to counteract any intoxicating effects: with the latter article we took care to stuff the lining of our coats, no haversacks being brought with us on this expedition.

Trudging off again through the snow, guided faithfully by the sticks, we had just arrived at the last one, when an officer of engineers appeared, accompanied by two of his men. He immediately desired us, in an authoritative manner, to go back with him to the block-house, and we, of course, were forced to comply with the command, although our reluctance was great, for more than one reason. Entering the house once more, the officer, by way of a great favour to us all, ordered one of his men to saw a barrel asunder; part of the contents of the same rum-keg we had been at was then poured into the empty half barrel: this unwieldy glass was raised to our heads with some difficulty.

Having thus regaled us with rum, he extended his generosity so far as to bid us fill our foraging-caps with biscuits; we did so, chuckling inwardly at the same time at having anticipated him: but on his pointing significantly to a heap of shovels and pickaxes, and ordering us to carry them to the village, the cause of his courtesy was cleared up at once. Heaving up our burdens, we set off, groaning under their weight: one of the engineers having become inebriated, he fell with his load, and rolled over the snow, losing at the same time his cargo of implements. This fellow's tongue consoled us, in some degree, for the officer's scurvy trick: he was so far from being awed by his commander, that he never failed to pour out volleys of abuse on him, at every interlude between the acts of rolling and rising up: this odd scene continued the whole way to the village, the officer stomaching all with astonishing meekness.

In the beginning of November, the plan for the invasion of France was put into execution. On the 8th of that month our brigade broke up from Roncesvalles, and marched again towards the heights of Mayo: the remainder of Hill's army had moved off before us; we were therefore necessitated to advance hastily to the place of destination. The roads were horrible, and the way long; but no rest was given till the object was attained: snatching a hurried meal, we threw ourselves exhausted on the ground. The force collected here was numerous in our estimation, consisting of no less than 110,000 men, British, Portuguese, and Spaniards.

Two hours after dark, the whole Allied Army began to descend into France: after marching for some time, a rivulet was crossed—a glimpse was then caught of a French Army, posted on the heights of Nivelle. They were instantly attacked, and the engagement became general: our brigade, however, was not troubled with firing a single shot, in consideration of their late harassing march, which the rest of the army had not endured, at least for some time previous. While this short action was going on, we remained in Reserve, perfectly indifferent to the animated scene before our eyes;—so much had excessive fatigue benumbed our curiosity.

A gleam of sunshine, the first we had seen for some time, now shone forth; and, stretching ourselves on the ground, the genial warmth was enjoyed as long as it lasted. The enemy having been discomfited, we took possession of their camp for the night. Certainly, this camp was the most magnificent I had ever beheld; the exertions of both nature and art had been lavished upon it in profusion. A party of French had taken the advantage of our absence from Mayo to carry off some baggage, which had been left behind; but the activity of Mina, the celebrated Spanish chief, prevented any other damage from being done.

The army continued to advance unmolested on this powerful country, which had so long successfully resisted the approach of the invader. After some days of exposure to heavy rains, our division reached the deserted town of Cambo, situated on the River Nive. Here we were quartered: the rest of the army were cantoned along the river; the French were also posted on its opposite side. Our regiment was strengthened at this place by the arrival of a draft.

One day Wellington appeared in the town, and surveyed its situation and neighbourhood. We all knew that this was the prelude to fighting, and prepared accordingly. On the same day the French sent down a regimental band to the edge of the river, and we listened attentively to every air they played. But next morning we rose before daylight, in expectation of another sort of music: our whole army was in busy commotion, preparing to pass the river.

Leaving Cambo, our brigade marched up to a ford: the right wing of the 71st then lined the river and commenced firing, as did the other portions of the army at the several crossing points. But, confining myself more minutely to our brigade's operations—the left wing entered the river under cover of the heavy fire, and attained the opposite bank; the 50th and 92nd followed their example—and lastly, the right wing. Thus, we found ourselves safe on *terra firma* again, without experiencing any greater loss than that of having a bugler wounded! The resistance of the enemy was equally faint along the other parts of the river: in fact, they were distracted by the noise and extent of the different attacks.

Next morning Hill's army moved on towards Bayonne: we

quartered ourselves for two days in its neighbourhood. Wellington's army had in the meantime retired across the Nive. The absence of such a large body of men encouraged Marshal Soult to issue from Bayonne, in hopes of crushing us before assistance could arrive; This movement brought on the Battle of Bayonne, in which our division alone succeeded in defeating Soult, before Wellington's succours could come up.

The success, however, was dearly purchased, by a loss of 2,000 men killed and wounded—among whom the 71st had a respectable number. For my part, I had not the honour of playing a part in the engagement, being all the while humbly employed in guarding General Barnes's baggage. In the course of the day the general received a wound, as did each of his *aides-de-camp*, the Captains Hamilton: the brothers were brought to the rear, and orders given for us guardsmen to bear them to a village at some distance.

After placing the wounded gentlemen in blankets, we waded off through the midst of a knee-deep muddy road. Setting all boasting aside, I sincerely declare that the battle's hottest moment would have been infinitely more pleasant to me, and less degrading, than this errand: the opinion of the other bearers was, I believe, much the same. Arriving at the village, application was made for admittance at the first good-looking house that appeared. This request was haughtily refused by a diminutive-looking sergeant of the 36th, who stood in the portal with a seeming determination to oppose our passage, and saying, "This is my colonel's house." Too tired to spend more time in expostulation, we pushed the little man fairly aside, entered the house, and placed the captains in beds.

On the ensuing day I was despatched with a letter to our brigade-major. Travelling alone, I fell inadvertently into a deep ditch by the way—so deep, indeed, that I did not feel its bottom, on account of being fortunate enough to lay hold of a bramble bush in the descent. Grasping desperately at this support, I hung on, with my head only out of water, in no enviable state of mind or body either, as may be supposed. Happily, as I thought, some

Spanish muleteers came in sight, approaching towards the ditch. I called loudly for their assistance: they raised their heads and gave me a vacant stare, continuing all the while to trot past very composedly, without slackening the pace of a single mule.

Whether it was indignation at such barbarous behaviour, or that Providence lent me aid, I will not decide; but at any rate I scrambled out, with no other damage than being completely drenched. Had not my firelock been in the same condition, I should at all events, have, made a ball hiss about the ears of the cold-blooded miscreants.

Shortly after I joined the regiment, the army advanced towards the River Adour. We were then often billeted upon country houses. Once, when some officers were in one of them, and six of us in the adjoining stable (which, by the by, we had some trouble in converting into a sleeping chamber, on account of the floor being luxuriantly bestrewed with mire), a discovery was made of a kind which rejoices the generality of mankind. One of the men going about a pile of faggots in the yard, was attracted, by the peculiarity of its construction, to pull down some of the wood and step into the midst of the pile: soon after, he cried for a bayonet, then a straw: these were handed in: the next accents were, "I have found a whole barrel of brandy!"

When the discoverer had satisfied himself, we went in, and sucked through the straw by turns; taking the utmost care, at the same time, to escape the officers' observation, for obvious reasons. As fate would have it, however, a soldier from another house suddenly entered the yard, for the purpose of visiting us. We received him as placidly as possible; but he must have either remarked our anxious glances at the faggots, or heard the fidgeting of the man who was amusing himself with the straw: perhaps both causes urged the prying stranger to run to the aperture and find out the mystery: thus he compelled us, as it were, to, "go snacks" with him.

After we had retired to roost in the stable, this ungrateful fellow divulged the secret to his comrades, and guided them to the spot: what they did there may be guessed; but in addition, they had slipped off and left the spigot of the barrel on the ground, by which means the liquor rushed furiously from the hole, and nearly overflowed the yard. The gurgling sound awakened me in the middle of the night: we got up and stopped the running, but it was almost too late. Next morning, when we came back from parade, the powerful effluvia of the spilt brandy was sensibly felt: this alarmed us not a little.

The certainty of being called to account for the transgression, prevailed in every bosom; and the idea of the officers' olfactory nerves winding the smell, was never once doubted. But, by a lucky thought, our terror and the smell were quashed together, by merely turning wet straw and mire over the dreaded places. The process was disgusting enough, to be sure; but the complete success of the scheme smoothed all the wrinkles of aversion.

We now marched to the banks of the Adour, and from thence to the town of Ort, on the same river, where our quarters were established till the month of February. The causes of this delay were derived from various circumstances, such as heavy rains, and the consequent dreadful state of the roads: indeed, the condition of the muleteers was a convincing proof of this, these men coming into the town regularly so bespattered with mud, that they had actually more the appearance of being composed of clay than of the ordinary human materials—which, by the by, are also called clay. But the kind I allude to was of a different description—it only covered the surface of the muleteers' persons: this crust, however, might have been several inches in depth.

We ourselves did not escape the miry contagion, on account of the very severe duty which all of us were liable to on this post. There was seldom even time to doff our garments, to say nothing of washing them in the usual manner. We generally pursued the antediluvian system of washing, that is to say, walking into a river, and scrubbing only externally—yet, strange as it may seem, colds or coughs were almost unknown to us: the constant exposure to fresh air will perhaps account for this.

Some French gunboats used to take advantage of dark nights, to pass the town, in their course to and from Bayonne: in daylight, or even moonlight, they never appeared. Although the French sailors took the precaution of using muffled oars, our pickets were too vigilant not to harass them by a random fire: this sometimes drew a return shot from the gunboats. The house where our captain lodged was once struck by a weighty ball—it passed through a clock-case, and drove in the wall of the room where the captain lay in bed, nearly burying him in a shower of mortar and rubbish.

One day the enemy landed on a small island on the Adour, where three of our companies were posted. After a smart contest, our men were driven by superior numbers from a large *château*, which in fact was the only defensible place in the island.

That night 100 of us crossed over to their support. From the quietness of the enemy, thoughts already began to be entertained that they had quitted the island; but to set the matter at rest, a patrol was detached to reconnoitre the *château*. They soon returned to say that it was deserted. Relying upon the idea of our former suspicions being right, a picket of twenty men was sent to occupy the *château*; whence five of us were sub-detached, to quarter ourselves in a farmhouse, which had formerly been used as a sort of outpost.

By mere chance, a man of our small party happened be on terms of intimacy with a girl of the house which we were going to. When we arrived at the place of destination, he therefore led the way, and tapped at the window—the same, I presume, that he had before lurked about, on a different errand from the present one. After some interrogation, the casement was softly opened; the girl and her mother then appeared: a serious conversation immediately commenced between them and the gallant, who spoke the French language very fluently, from his having been once a prisoner.

We scarcely understood a single word; but it was easy to perceive that symptoms of strong alarm were depicted on the countenances of the females. At length it was interpreted to us, that a strong party of French soldiers were quartered in a house only a few yards distant! This intelligence surprised us a little; but being unwilling to retrace our steps in such a dark tempestuous night, we stood irresolutely pondering whether to remain or fly. The young woman now offered to go to the dreaded house, on some pretext or other, and ascertain the number of the foes. She went accordingly, and soon returned, after having discovered that they consisted of an officer and sixty men.

Reckless of the danger, however, we entered the house, and expressed our determination to keep snug till the morning, notwithstanding the good creatures' entreaties for us to save ourselves. Indeed, such unaffected anxiety for our preservation astonished us not a little; and what could be a nobler instance of courageous hospitality than the peasant girl's not delivering us into the hands of her countrymen? She realised, in fact, the masculine though fictitious heroines of the Waverley novels.

We had taken the precaution of placing a sentinel under a tree: when this duty came to my turn, I could perceive a French sentinel close by me, walking to and fro in the usual manner. He stopped once—I grasped my musquet firmer;—but it was to light his pipe with a flint and steel: a great noise and jabbering could also be heard, which arose from the Frenchmen in the house. Before daylight came in, we prudently resolved to steal off; but in the execution of this, our good fortune only partially continued; the enemy observing us and giving chase, firing at the same time several shots.

But trusting to our heels, we soon gained the *château*, where the fifteen men were already stationed at the windows, ready to repel any assault, they having been roused by the musquetry of the pursuers: but they, on the other hand, seemed to have stopped in their career, and evacuated the island, as we saw them no more.

I have mentioned the boisterous weather we had endured ever since the invasion of France. People who have been accustomed to read of the "laughing climate" of the south of France, will scarcely recognise my poor description to be of the identical part which is so heavenly in their imaginations. To be sure, it must be allowed that the winter of 1814 was severe through the whole of Europe; but the glowing accounts of southern French, Spanish, and Italian winters are in general false: their summers are indeed different from ours; yet, after all, the climate of the whole earth is, in my humble opinion, more alike than most travellers care to own.

CHAPTER 9

A Galling Discovery

The month of February saw the Allied Army again in readiness to push its conquests further into France. Our brigade left Ort, and after having had a slight skirmish with the enemy, we marched on till the evening, and encamped. A French store lying exposed in the neighbourhood, some of the men entered it, and possessed themselves of a quantity of bread. I was first warned of this by seeing the depredators hurrying along, each bearing an immense loaf: the 92nd men had theirs wrapped up in the tails of their kilts! In the impulse of the moment, I ran down to the store, but at a most unlucky time, the brigade-major having just arrived.

On perceiving him, I stopped short, and immediately retreated, with as unconcerned an air as possible; this would not do, however; the major was too sharp not to discern the purport of my errand—so raising his voice, he called for me to halt. But lending a deaf ear to the command, I only increased my pace—upon which the vindictive major put spurs to his horse, with the hope of seizing me. My being overtaken was now certain, had I not had the presence of mind to ascend a rugged hilly path, impervious to the horse: this stratagem saved me. It was then I had time to blame myself for running headlong into such a scrape; and, perhaps, the idea of still wanting a loaf did not tend to decrease my chagrin.

On the following morning our army moved off; two companies of us, the German Riflemen, and the light companies of the other regiments, being in advance. It was drawing near night when the enemy were discovered posted along the brow of a mountain, upon which we, the light troops, sat down on the face of a rising ground—the rest of the army halting at the same time. The hostilities of the day commenced by the British artillery making several discharges upon the enemy. From the contiguity of the surrounding hills, the reports of the cannon were of the loudness of thunder.

Perhaps it was this circumstance that induced an Irish officer of ours to express himself thus: "Blood an' ouns, Mister M—d, are these our kenun!" On Mr. M—d assuring the brave lieutenant that they were, he seemed much comforted. This *jontleman* was at all times the standing joke of the regiment, chiefly from his uncouth form and tremendous brogue,—another example of which may be given. Seeing a sergeant with a telescope in his hand, he accosted him in this manner: "Och, *sarjant*, will you lend me the loan of your spy-horn glass!"

But to return from the vagaries of the poor Patlander. The light companies were now ordered to advance upon the enemy: we did so, and met their light troops, or *tirailleurs*, half-way between the respective armies. A severe skirmishing then took place. This system of fighting is of course already well known; but I may say, that although the combatants are in a scattered state, and take aim at each other, yet they very seldom know when they drop their men—to speak in sportsmen's slang. The reason is obvious;—so many firing at the same time, and that often obliquely.

In this, as well as in other skirmishes, we had occasion to admire the steady coolness of the German riflemen: these fellows never took the pipe out of their mouths, but fired away, as if they were only engaged at some ordinary occupation. The *tirailleurs* continued to retire gradually before us, and eventually fled for protection to their main body. Our enthusiasm not permitting us to wait for support, we rushed up the hill, regardless of the heavy fire which the enemy poured down from the top of it: when that part of the mountain was attained, they descended on the opposite side. By this time, it was quite dark; we halted accordingly: the rest of the division then came up and encamped. Our loss was less than might have been expected from such a smart brush.

Next morning 100 of us were detached to a village, for the purpose of observing the enemy, who were posted on the opposite side of a river. We stood for a considerable time in the village street, which gave the French inhabitants an opportunity of displaying their usual benevolence. They actually came out, took the canteens off our backs, and replaced, them full of wine. When our commanding officer endeavoured to prevent such attentions, the worthy people watched till his back was turned, and then resumed. How different was this from the conduct of some French soldiers! disregarding the ordinary *punctilios* of war, they fired across the river, and shot one of the 13th Dragoons dead in our sight. This unfortunate man was on guard.

Our indignation at this action was no way decreased on seeing another dragoon, a young Englishman, burst into tears at the fall of his comrade: he hung over the lifeless body for a long while, absorbed in grief, telling us also that the deceased had been as a father to him, and that the poor man had been upwards of twenty years in the regiment, respected by all who knew him.

General Stewart now came up, and took forty of us across the river. While fording, we observed the water to be full of flour in bags: the enemy had probably thrown them there, to prevent their falling into the hands of the British. Nothing of importance resulted from this reconnoitring. On our coming to a place where two roads struck off, I was stationed, along with other five men, to guard one of them: the rest of the party advanced along the other road, so far as to skirmish with the enemy, and to suffer a loss of two men, who were made prisoners. The division soon afterwards forded the river and joined us.

Marching on again towards Salvaterre, we came in sight of another river, with the enemy drawn up, along its banks. Our artillery immediately opened a dreadful fire upon their ranks, under cover of which the 92nd and two of our companies entered the river. It was about this time that General Hill's horse was killed by a cannon-ball. The general falling along with the animal, in sight of almost the whole division, a momentary gleam of concern passed over every countenance: but this was soon dispelled by his rising up unhurt. The death of General Hill would have undoubtedly been deplored by us all, so universally was he esteemed: in short, the highest eulogy that can be paid him is to say that he was no way inferior to General Stewart in true greatness of soul and goodness of heart.

The 92nd having arrived on the opposite shore, and the rest of the division being busily employed passing the river on the beams of a wooden bridge, the planks of which had been taken away, the enemy took to their heels: we then occupied a village for that and the following day. Continuing our march, not a day passed over without skirmishes taking place. Fording, also, formed a necessary but troublesome part of our labour, this district of France being intersected with innumerable streams.

At one time, while preparing to cross a very rapid one, a tall fellow must needs display his wit at the expense of another, whose stature could not be much vaunted of, saying, that he would carry him over dry, by fastening him to his brush and pricker. But, after all, it was amusing enough to find that the wit was the only one in the whole regiment that required assistance, he having stumbled, and been saved from drowning only through the exertions of his comrades.

Arriving in the vicinity of Orthes, we encamped within a mile of the River Gave. Soult had now concentrated his army in front of Orthes, with the hope of stopping our farther progress. One day we made a feint by marching along the stream; but it was not till the following day that the intention of crossing was put into execution. Wellington's army was entrusted with the attack of the enemy's right and centre, while we were ordered to do as much for their left, which was commanded by General Clausel. Marching, accordingly, towards the Gave, we crossed it under cover of both artillery and musquetry, with so much success as to have only one of the 71st wounded; the other regiments of the division suffering equally little. Continuing our march, we arrived at the summit of a rising ground, and there halted.

Close by us stood a house and a small wood: out of these sheltered places a party of French kept up a galling fire;—the men were falling every moment: this threw everyone into a sort of fidgety state of anxiety to close with the enemy;—in fact, unseen, destroyers generally produce such an effect. Two companies of our regiment at length received permission to chastise the lurkers; and instantly rushing down, they drove them out of the wood in a few seconds. The remainder of the enemy in the house were as yet unaware how things stood with their comrades of the wood.

This gave an opportunity for a young lad, named Jack, to take his station at the side of the house-door. The eyes of the whole brigade were now fixed upon the movements of the robust youth, when one of our band-men, suddenly breaking loose from those who endeavoured to restrain him, ran down to the house, wielding a stretching-pole, and placed himself on the other side of the door.

The unsuspecting Frenchmen at length began to issue from the door, unconscious of the fate that waited them. Immediately, Jack, with his firelock, and M'Rae with his pole, laid every one that appeared sprawling on the ground: if any were so fortunate as to escape the gun; they infallibly felt the weight of the pole; and *vice versâ*. A number of prisoners were thus secured, by the mere exertions of these two! Jack was made a corporal upon the spot; but poor M'Rae went unrewarded, he having little more than his valour to recommend him.

Moving on again, we came to a small village, where some partial skirmishing enlivened the scene. Our brigade then formed into close column. Soon after this evolution, a body of troops came in sight, advancing along a road: their steps were hasty and agitated; but they were suffered to pass us unmolested, we making no doubt of their being Spaniards. It was not long, however, before the mistake was rather unsatisfactorily explained, by

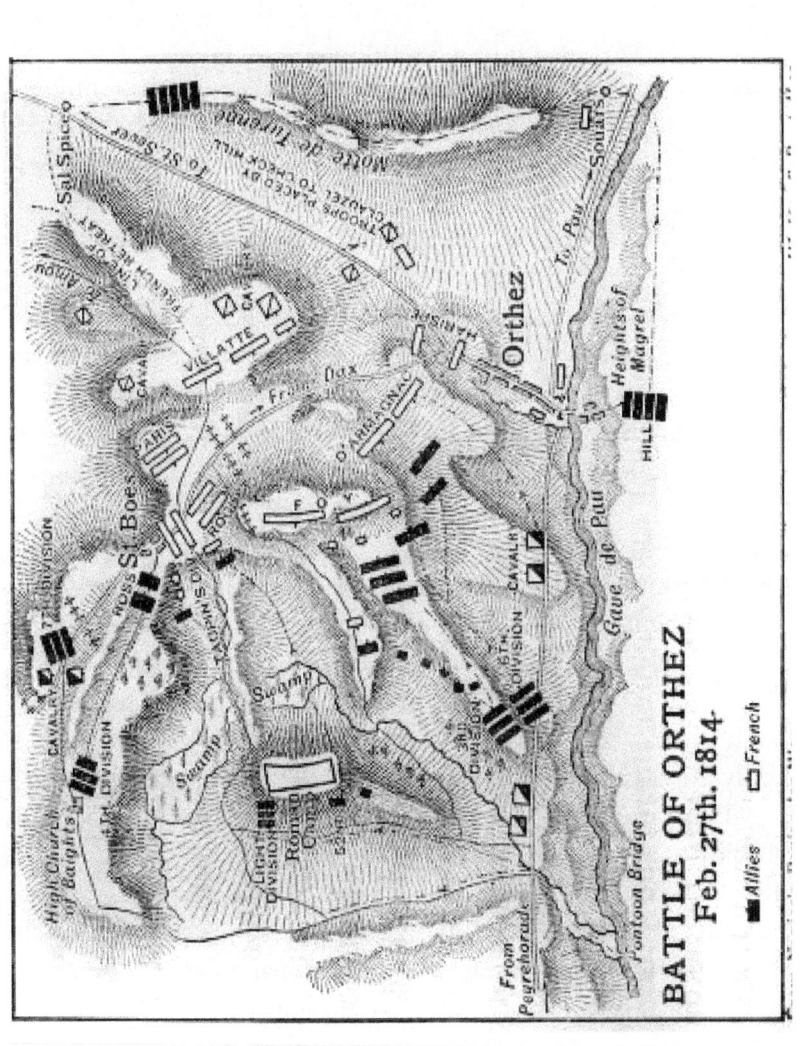

the appearance of a Scottish brigade (the 42nd, 79th, and 91st,) coming down the same road, playing furiously on their pipes, in full cry of the French, our supposed Spaniards. This discovery galled us to the quick; the fugitives having been completely at our mercy.

But if they escaped from the infantry, they did not from the British cavalry; for, on looking round, we could see the country covered, as far as the eye could reach, with the broken and flying enemy: our horsemen were following them close, committing dreadful havoc upon such as did not halt and throw down their arms. The field of Orthes having thus been decided, we encamped for the night, and next morning pursued our march; passing, as usual, quantities of military wrecks. I remarked, in particular, a place where several roads united: here immense heaps, or rather hills, of knapsacks, belts, caps, and canteens, lay piled on each other: they had, probably, been thrown down by the enemy that they might accelerate their flight.

At one time, a number of us happening to be quartered on a farmhouse, its inmates supplied the most rapacious of our band, gratuitously, with a quantity of bread. A hen-roost, which stood in the yard, excited much attention: its inhabitants were, I believe, roughly treated; nay, even a sergeant was detected by the farmer in the very act of twisting a fowl's neck: Stripes was a little nonplussed at the rencontre; but having the presence of mind to say that he had found a dead hen, the honest, farmer only good-humouredly replied, that "it must have died *per force!*"

The night before the Battle of Aire took place, while a number of us were carousing over abundance of wine and brandy, R——h, an intimate friend of mine, remained alone, gloomy and silent: we were the more surprised at this, as he had been always, hitherto, the blithest of a jolly company. On the following day, while we were advancing to engage the French, I walked alongside of him, but still he was morose and unaccountably silent; in fact, his former free and generous temper seemed to, be entirely gone. We now parted—alas! for ever. The troops having halted for a short time, General Stewart desired a sergeant to place a sentinel at the gate of a large *château* which stood hard by; and this job falling to my lot, the general ordered me to admit none but General Hill's staff.

Meanwhile, the Generals Hill and Stewart entered into deep conversation; *aides-de-camp* were continually passing out and in, bringing and carrying intelligence. One of them I particularly remarked—Colonel Hood, of the Guards; he was often examining a chart of the country, in addition to his other duties: this gentleman was soon afterwards slain in the engagement.

During this animated scene, an elderly Frenchman, an inmate of the *château*, scraped an acquaintance with me by asking for a small bit of tobacco. Having immediately gratified his request, the "faithful old domestic" disappeared, and soon returned, bearing a large loaf and a jug of wine. The loaf being too unwieldy to go into my haversack in a lump, he took the trouble to break it down piece-meal, and cram it into the bag. As this action would have seemed improper in the eyes of the two generals, the old man carefully hid his treat when their faces were in our direction, and pretended to look at the army; but the instant their backs were turned, he continued his kind exertions.

The division having at length moved off, and my business being ended, I ran hastily on to join the regiment, taking short cuts through some fields to effect this the sooner. The noise of musquetry beginning to burst on my ear, I did not relax in speed till a river stopped the way; but seeing a horseman fording it, I followed him, and reached the opposite shore in safety, after having been once nearly swept away. Joining the regiment in the midst of a severe skirmish, I was surprised to see one of our men with a long red feather stuck in his cap: on asking him the cause, I was informed that the unfortunate R——h had fallen a victim to the first shot in the engagement, and that he (the informant) had succeeded in shooting the French grenadier who had done the deed: the seizure of this man's feather was, therefore, intended as a sort of proof of revenge;—another instance of deadly forboding was thus exemplified.

The skirmishing continued still to rage with unabated fury:

it is to be understood, however, that our force consisted only of two 71st companies and the light companies of the other regiments; the rest of the division having gone to attack the main body of the enemy, who were posted upon a range of hills. I was, as usual, fortunate this day, having only received a ball through my trowsers; another tore up the ground, underneath my shoe: the latter accident made some around me conjecture that I had at length caught a wound—they were deceived, however, and I had still the appellation of "lucky." Indeed, a *fétiche* would always have been a superfluous article with me.

Our opponents having been worsted, towards nightfall it was agreed that we should quarter ourselves in the town of Aire, the rest of the division being encamped at some distance, on the field of battle. This part of the army had succeeded in routing the enemy, after an arduous conflict, in which M'Rae, our heroic musician, fell to rise no more. This strange being was far from possessing the ordinary coolness of Scotchmen. Although his profession absolved him from intermixing with the combatants—yet, on hearing the noise, of an engagement, he seemed to be seized with an irresistible fury, catching up a pole or a firelock, and rushing into the thickest of the fight, dealing blows with the greatest force and efficiency.

But fate cut short his career at Aire: he had there even exceeded his former valorous exploits, having levelled many a foe with the aid of his trusty pole; but just as he was poising it on high; to ensure a weighty blow upon a French soldier's skull, the man anticipated him, by firing the shot which stretched him lifeless in the dust. Certainly it may be said of the doughty M'Rae, that "swords he smiled at, weapons laughed to scorn."

On entering Aire, the first conspicuous objects that struck our eyes were two carts full to the brim of hams: little ceremony was used in helping ourselves to them all! No billets were served out here, everyone entering the house that suited him best: but the inhabitants bore the oppression with great good-nature. In the house where I was lodged, along with some others, the people pointed out to us some clean beds to repose upon; but as we had been ordered not to take off our accoutrements, the offer was refused: whether or not, our tremendously muddy state would have prevented us from trespassing so far on their politeness as to befoul the beds. We made ourselves very comfortable on the floor, with the help of a little straw.

Next day we marched out of the town to join our respective regiments, and had the trouble of coming back along with them. The streets of Aire were strewed with the bodies of French soldiers, who had been wounded in the divers engagements, and had had only strength to drag themselves into the town—there to die.

At one time, an officer of ours, a Mr. Cox, said to me, that I might take as many men as I chose to go out and bury R——h; but a pioneer, overhearing the discourse, assured us that he had buried the poor fellow:—this serves to shew how much the deceased was esteemed by men of all ranks in the regiment.

Having been joined by a draft of 200, we left Aire, and journeyed towards Pau: after halting a day or two in its neighbourhood, a movement was made in the direction of Toulouse. We made an attempt to lay a pontoon bridge over the Garonne, but without success: we were obliged to construct it farther up the river. A long march was next provided for us, and we returned to the place of starting, after marching at least fifty miles without resting—but perhaps this walk was necessary to alarm the enemy. We next marched to a place within two miles of Toulouse, where the inhabitants had fled, their wine-cellars remained, however, of which many of us could have given a minute description.

On the morning of the 10th of April, we advanced towards the city, or rather the St. Cyprien suburbs, which, are situated on the west bank of the Garonne. The enemy had a battery of ship guns here, which were sometimes discharged at us, but with poor effect; in fact, it may be said of our division, that only a few light companies were engaged. Wellington's army having crossed to the Toulouse side of the river, by far the hottest part of the engagement raged there: from morning till night, we had little more to do than listen to tremendous firing. It is said that the Spaniards behaved with astonishing bravery; they had certainly much need to do so, if it were for no other reason than to wipe off their former reproach. To make a long story short, the battle of Toulouse terminated in favour of the British: thus, Soult's last expiring blow completely failed.

Next morning the division marched through the city immense crowds of well-dressed people stood at a bridge to welcome us, or at least pretended to do so: all of them wore white cockades. Another group was busily employed in pulling down a statue of Napoleon from the top of a triumphal arch. As we advanced farther into the place, almost every window was filled by ladies waving handkerchiefs. Fortunately for the 60th and 92nd, they had lately got new clothes—their appearance, therefore, was passable in the eyes of the French; but as for us and most of the other regiments, anything like magnificent costume was out of the question.

Our clothes were in fact worn out; but not a rag hung, pennant-like, in the air, strict orders having been issued to that effect, although full liberty had been given to mend the holes with any sort of cloth. This indulgence was acted up to in the fullest extent—patches of canvass and of blankets covering us from head to foot, interspersed throughout with other patches, of all the colours of the rainbow: such habiliments had a very harlequin, mendicant effect.

With regard to our personal appearance, many were tanned and weather-beaten by the long exposure to sun, frost, and rain; but the late drafts, of course, were much less so. I may remark here, that the Portuguese were now much finer-looking soldiers than the generality of the British: the cause of this arose from the immense number of striplings who filled the ranks of the latter, while the Portuguese were almost wholly composed of full-grown, sturdy fellows.

On emerging from Toulouse, we directed our steps to the side of the Languedoc canal, and there encamped. While on parade at another place, intelligence arrived of the northern allies' entry into Paris, and the subsequent deposition of Napoleon. This news diffused universal joy: a busy hum of delight ran round every rank; home and friends only were talked of—for who cared a fig for the affairs of France? But still in expectation of fighting, we moved on to Ville Franche; old Soult being as yet resolved to consider us enemies to his country. Such conduct in a Blucher has been denominated "heroic patriotism;" but in our opponent it received the name of "stubbornness," or "a thirst of blood."

A flag of truce at length arriving for the suspension of all hostilities, we marched back to Toulouse. Our stay in this city extended to about six weeks: the whole of this time was spent in the most agreeable manner, the inhabitants being friendly—the provisions and liquor "dog-cheap." One night an illumination was ordered; but it turned out to be of a very paltry description—a single candle in each window forming the average number of lights.

Preparations being made for the public entry of the Duc d'Angoulême, our brigade, with some Portuguese, were called out to assist the National Guards in lining the streets. It must be understood. however, that we had exchanged our former scarecrow dresses for good substantial clothing, previous to this "august ceremony."

People of rank are well aware how much their importance is increased by the easy method of keeping the mobility, for days or hours, in momentary expectation of their arrival: the truth of this we and a large crowd besides found, having stood from morning till the approach of dusk, waiting the duke's arrival. The duke at last appeared, surrounded by an immense suite of officers, both French and British: they passed under a triumphal arch erected for the occasion. A faint cheering was heard at times among the citizens, but the National Guards were extremely vociferous—however, the subject is too stale to admit of comment.

We had another job in lining the streets, on account of a grand ball being given to the British officers and French nobility. When the duke was leaving Toulouse, we turned out and saluted him: that day chanced to be the anniversary of the Battle of Fuentes de Honoro; every one of us had, therefore, a sprig of laurel stuck in his cap. I have little doubt but that the poor duke considered these decorations intended solely to do him honour.

Twelve of us were once hired to perform dumb parts in a theatre; this was assuredly my first and last debut. When the place was reached, we were all gorgeously dressed, the play being some grand eastern spectacle or other. Our first labour was to bear a princess across the stage in a *palanquin*, or at least in one of those gilded hand-barrows which pass, for such in playhouses: some of us also wielded formidable-looking tin pikes, as the princess's guards. But the most comical part of our operations was, to be furnished with wooden instruments, and perched on a balcony, to have the resemblance of a second orchestra.

We did everything in our power to aid the views of the manager, by seeming to blow with great musical taste upon his instruments: one fellow, in particular, aped the actions of a musician in the most ridiculous manner, such as beating with his foot, twirling his fingers, and making sundry other contortions. All the while, an entire dependence was placed upon the real theatrical orchestra for concealing the imposture by their noise and skill.

In our manoeuvres of the stage, we were very much assisted in comprehending the actors' directions, by the interpretations of a French sea-officer, who had acquired the English language in a prison: he had apparently volunteered his services to the theatre for that night. Among the spectators we recognised several British officers; but I scarcely think they knew us in our new profession.

Preparations began now to be made for our final departure; several regiments had ere this time been despatched for America, and rumours were even afloat that that was our place of destination. The Spaniards and Portuguese who had enlisted in the British service were all dismissed: several of them belonged to our regiment. One Portuguese boy was allowed to remain, he having obstinately refused to leave us. The story of this youth is rather singular. In 1808, one of our officers hired him as a servant, and afterwards brought him to Glasgow, where the second battalion was quartered: here our hero fired with military ardour, enlisted with it, and was latterly sent out in a draft to Lisbon, his native city.

Previous to his joining us in the interior, the officers had actually been obliged to use force in compelling him to visit his parents, who were both alive. Such was his ambition to be considered a "Glasgow chap," that he never was heard to utter a syllable in either Spanish or Portuguese; in fact, he had determined to renounce his country, and make the headquarters of the 71st his home.

About this time, our honest Italian thought proper to decamp; he took his arms and accoutrements away, besides *borrowing* a watch from a sergeant. This odd character was afterwards seen in Paris by some 71st men; he was then in the Prussian service.

On the 5th of June we marched from Toulouse; a number of the inhabitants turned out to bid us farewell. It was soon found that the Italian was not the only deserter—many men being missing; chiefly, it was supposed, from the attractions or enticements of French women;—no less than twenty of our regiment were in this predicament.

Our march to Bourdeaux occupied seventeen days: during the whole of our way we were delighted with the richness of the country, and, above all, with the kindness of the people; often did they refuse payment for provisions and wine: although some of them appeared to be in indigent circumstances, yet they were as bountiful as their more opulent neighbours. Sometimes we were quartered in splendid gentlemen's seats or *châteaux*, where, upon being ushered into fine carpeted rooms, with gilded beds, the natural diffidence arising from our total ignorance of such luxuries made us often draw back involuntarily; but the inhabitants generally succeeded in politely forcing us to make ourselves at home.

I am no would-be liberal, nor do I wish to chime in, for

fashion's sake, with the present system of praising the French, in opposition to our old vulgar ideas of them; I only wish to state the truth, or, in other words, what I actually experienced. English, Scotch, or Irish hospitality may be talked of; I seldom if ever found any of it: it was in France that the true meaning of the word was realised to us.

After passing through Bourdeaux, we marched to Blanchefort camp, where a number of other regiments were waiting for vessels to convey them home. In addition to the good market which was established here, innumerable carts came out from Bourdeaux loaded with wine and brandy: their drivers kept up such an incessant noise in the camp, by the calling of "Rhum," that sentinels were placed to prevent their entrance. By the word rhum, or rum, they intended that we should understand brandy. Frenchmen were not the only liquor-merchants; an Aberdeen smack having arrived, with a quantity of porter on board—the "pawky" crew came to the camp, and sold it at a *franc* per bottle, which was exactly the price of brandy; however, the muddy beverage was much run upon from its rarity.

In making a calculation of our numbers, it was found, that out of the 600 picked men who went to Portugal in 1810 only 75 remained, I do not mean to say that every individual out of this mighty deficiency was actually dead; some were in existence, but in a disabled state, although perhaps not just "at the town's end for life." In the month of July 1814, we embarked at Poliac in transports, and were conveyed to the mouth of the Garonne, where the whole regiment, and two companies of the 50th, were put on board of the *Sultan*, of 74 guns. In the short space of five days the Cove of Cork was reached. Six precious years had elapsed since I left this place, in a company of 100 men, in the prime of youth. Of these, only three men and myself now returned!

Historical Record of the Seventy-First Regiment Highland Light Infantry (Extract)

By Richard Cannon

In March 1808, the regiment proceeded from Middleton to Cork, where its equipment in every respect was completed.

The second battalion embarked at Londonderry for Scotland on the 9th of April 1808, after transferring 200 men to the first battalion, which raised the strength of the latter to nearly 900 rank and file.

The Peninsula was at this period the centre of political interest. Portugal, deserted by her government, and Spain betrayed, the people of each rose in arms to recover the national independence. Dissensions had arisen in the royal family of Spain, occasioned by the sway of Emanuel Godoy, who bore the title of Prince of Peace. This minister was dismissed, but the court was unable to restore tranquillity. In this emergency, the French emperor was solicited to be umpire, and Napoleon ultimately placed the crown of Spain on his brother Joseph, who was transferred from the throne of Naples.

The Spaniards flew to arms in consequence. The British government resolved to aid the Spanish and Portuguese patriots, and a British Army was ordered to proceed to the Peninsula, under the command of Lieut.-General Sir Arthur Wellesley. The first battalion of the Seventy-First regiment formed part of the force selected on this occasion.

The first battalion of the Seventy-First regiment embarked

at the Cove of Cork on the 17th of June 1808. Its strength consisted of fifty-two sergeants, twenty-two drummers, and eight hundred and seventy-four rank and file.

In June 1808 His Majesty King George III. was pleased to approve of the Seventy-First bearing the title of Glasgow regiment, in addition to the appellation of Highland regiment.

In the first instance, the Seventy-First were brigaded with the fifth, thirty-eighth, and fifth battalion of the sixtieth regiment, under Brigadier-General Henry Fane, and sailed for Portugal, in conjunction with the forces destined to aid the Spaniards and Portuguese, on the 12th of July. After a favourable passage, the troops anchored in Mondego Bay in the beginning of August, and a landing was effected in the vicinity of the village of Frejus.

Early in the morning of the 4th of August a small piquet of the enemy stationed in the neighbourhood fell back, and the operation of disembarking the troops was carried into effect without opposition. The army then moved on to a position across a deep sandy country, where it halted, and encamped for the night.

At this period a change took place in the arrangement of the brigades, and the first battalion of the Seventy-First was placed, with the thirty-sixth and fortieth regiments, in that commanded by Major-General Ronald Craufurd Ferguson.

The division under Major-General Sir Brent Spencer, K.B., from Cadiz, consisting of about four thousand men, joined on the 8th of August; and, after a short halt, the army was again put in motion to occupy a more forward position, where it remained for some days. On the 17th of August the enemy, commanded by General Laborde, was encountered near Roileia. The position was attacked, and carried with great loss to the French, who retreated on Torres Vedras.

The light company of the Seventy-First was the only part of the regiment engaged, the remainder being employed in manoeuvring on the right flank of the French. The light company suffered a trifling loss, having but one man killed and a few wounded.

The Seventy-First subsequently received the Royal Authority to bear the word "Roleia" on the regimental colour and appointments, in commemoration of this victory.

Lieut.-General Sir Arthur Wellesley, after the Battle of Roleia, did not pursue the enemy by the high roads, but keeping to the right near the sea, marched to Vimiera, to cover the landing of a brigade commanded by Major-General Anstruther, which was effected on the 20th of August.

The morning of the 21st of August was given up to the troops, in order to prepare and repose themselves. The men were engaged in washing and cleaning their equipments, when the approach of the enemy, moving to the left, was discovered at eight o'clock in the morning, and the brigades commanded by Major-General Ferguson, Brigadier-Generals Nightingall, Acland, and Bowes, were consequently moved across a valley from the heights on the west to those on the east of Vimiera.

Marshal Junot, Duke of Abrantes, moved on his army to the attack of the position, and commenced it on the British centre, where the fiftieth regiment was posted, moving along the front gradually to the left, until the whole line became engaged.

A short time previously to this, the soldiers of the brigade were ordered to sit down, with their arms in their hands, keeping their formation. The enemy in the meantime cannonaded the whole line, and pushed on his sharpshooters and infantry. To oppose the former, Major-General Ferguson ordered the left sections of companies to move forward and skirmish. Upon the retreat of the enemy's sharpshooters, the action became general along the front of this brigade, and the whole moved forward to the attack. Nothing could surpass the steadiness of the troops on this occasion, and the general and commanding officer set a noble example, which was followed by all.

The grenadier company of the Seventy-First greatly distinguished itself, in conjunction with a subdivision of the light company of the Thirty-Sixth regiment. Captain Alexander Forbes, who commanded the grenadier company, was ordered to the support of some British artillery, and, seizing a favourable

Piper Clark, 71st Highland Light Infantry

opportunity, made a dash at a battery of the enemy's artillery immediately in his front. He succeeded in capturing five guns and a howitzer, with horses, caissons, and equipment complete. In this affair alone the grenadier company had Lieutenants John Pratt and Ralph Dudgeon and thirteen rank and file wounded, together with two men killed.

★★★★★★★★★★

> Lieut.-General Sir Harry Burrard landed during the action, but did not assume the command. Lieut.-General Sir Hew Dalrymple landed on the following day, and took command of the army. The force under Lieut.-General Sir John Moore was also disembarked during the negotiation, which subsequently took place, making the British Army to amount to thirty-two thousand men.

★★★★★★★★★★

The French made a daring effort to retake their artillery, both with cavalry and infantry; but the gallant conduct of the grenadier company, and the advance of Major-General Ferguson's brigade, finally left the guns in the possession of those who had so gallantly captured them.

George Clark, one of the pipers of the regiment, and afterwards piper to the Highland Society of London, was wounded in this action, and being unable to accompany his corps in the advance against the enemy, put his pipes in order, and struck up a favourite regimental air, to the great delight of his comrades. This is the second instance in which the pipers of the Seventy-First have behaved with particular gallantry, and evinced high feeling for the credit and honour of the corps.

During the advance of the battalion, several prisoners were taken, among whom was the French general, Brennier. Corporal John McKay, of the Seventy-First, who took him, was afterwards promoted to an ensigncy in the Fourth West India Regiment.

The result of this battle was the total defeat of the enemy, who subsequently retreated on Lisbon, with the loss of twenty-one pieces of cannon, twenty-three ammunition waggons, with powder, shells, stores of all descriptions, and 20,000 rounds of musket ammunition, together with a great many officers and soldiers killed, wounded, and taken prisoners.

The conduct of the battalion, and of its commanding officer, Lieut.-Colonel Pack, was noticed in the public despatches, and the thanks of both Houses of Parliament were conferred on the troops.

The following officers of the Seventy-First were wounded in the Battle of Vimiera: Captains Arthur Jones and Maxwell Mackenzie; Lieutenants John Pratt, William Hartley, Augustus McIntyre, and Ralph Dudgeon; Ensign James Campbell, and Acting Adjutant R. McAlpin.

The Seventy-First subsequently received the Royal Authority to bear the word "Vimiera" on the regimental colour and appointments, in commemoration of this battle.

The "Convention of Cintra" was the result of this victory, and it was signed on the 30th of August. By its provisions the French Army evacuated Portugal, which country became freed from its oppressors.

The British Army was ordered to move forward to Lisbon, some of the reinforcements for it having preceded it by water, and occupied the forts at the mouth of the Tagus. The French Army having by this convention fallen back on Lisbon, the British proceeded to the vicinity of Fort St. Julien, and encamped.

All the objects of the expedition being carried into effect, and the French troops embarked for France, the British Army remained for some time at Lisbon and its vicinity. At this period (September) Lieut.-General Sir John Moore, having assumed the command, made dispositions for entering Spain.

The first battalion of the Seventy-First was now brigaded with the Thirty-Sixth and Ninety-Second regiments under Brigadier-General Catlin Craufurd, and placed in the division under the command of Lieut.-General the Honourable John Hope, afterwards the Earl of Hopetoun. On the 27th of October the division was put in motion, and after a short stay at Badajoz resumed the march, proceeding by Merida, Truxillo, Jaraicejo, Puerto-de-Merivette, and crossing the Tagus at the bridge of Almaraz, directed its route upon Talavera-de-la-Reyna. From this town the column proceeded to the Escurial, seven leagues to the north-west of Madrid.

Intelligence was here received of the enemy's approach towards Madrid, and two companies of the Seventy-First, under Major Archibald Campbell, were pushed forward to occupy the important pass in the Guadarama Mountains, which separate Old from New Castile. After a halt of a few days, the division was put in motion over the Guadarama Pass to Villa Castin, at which place Lieut.-General the Honourable John Hope, in consequence of the intelligence which he received of the enemy's movements, made a night march to the left, by Avila and Peneranda, and finally proceeded to Alba-de-Tormes.

At the latter place a junction was formed with a detachment from the army under Lieut.-General Sir John Moore, then at Salamanca. The army under Sir John Moore was shortly afterwards put in motion towards Valladolid, and subsequently to the left, to form a junction with Lieut.-General Sir David Baird's division, which had landed at Corunna.

Previously to this period, the Spanish Armies under General Blake, near Bilboa on the left, General Castanos in the centre, and General Palafox lower down the Ebro on the right, had been completely defeated; and Lieut.-General Sir John Moore consequently made arrangements for a retreat on Portugal by Ciudad Rodrigo; but it having been represented to him that Madrid held out against the French, he was induced to effect a junction with Lieut.-General Sir David Baird, in order to make a diversion in favour of Madrid, by attacking Marshal Soult on the River Carion.

The British force, twenty-nine thousand strong, joined at Toro on the 21st of December, and on the 23rd of that month Sir John Moore advanced with the whole army. The cavalry had already met with that of the enemy, and the infantry were within two hours' march of him, when an intercepted letter informed the British commander that Napoleon, who had entered Madrid on the 4th of December, was then in full march for Salamanca and Benevente. A retreat on Corunna, through

Gallicia, was immediately decided on, that through Portugal being then impracticable.

Accordingly, the several divisions marched towards the Esla, the greater part crossing by the bridge of Benevente on the 26th of December, when, after a day's halt, the cavalry under Lieut.-General Lord Paget and Brigadier-General the Honourable Charles Stewart had an engagement with some of the Imperial Guards that had forded the River Esla under General Le Fevre, who was made prisoner, with several of his men.

At this period the situation of the British Army was dispiriting in the extreme. In the midst of winter, in a dreary and desolate country, the soldiers, chilled and drenched with the heavy rains, and wearied by long and rapid marches, were almost destitute of fuel to cook their victuals, and it was with extreme difficulty that they could procure shelter. Provisions were scarce, irregularly issued, and difficult of attainment.

The waggons, in which were their magazines, baggage, and stores, were often deserted in the night by the Spanish drivers, who were terrified by the approach of the French. Thus baggage, ammunition, stores, and even money were destroyed to prevent them falling into the hands of the enemy; and the weak, the sick, and the wounded were necessarily left behind. The Seventy-First suffered in proportion with the rest, and by weakness, sickness, and fatigue lost about ninety-three men.

On the 5th of January 1809, a position was taken up at Lugo, where some skirmishing occurred, in which three companies of the Seventy-First were engaged, and repulsed the enemy.

Lieut.-General Francis Dundas was appointed from the Ninety-Fourth regiment to be Colonel of the Seventy-First on the 7th of January 1809, in succession to Lieut.-General Sir John Francis Cradock, K.B., removed to the Forty-Third regiment.

The retreat was again commenced on the 9th of January; and on the 11th the army, still nearly fifteen thousand strong, reached Corunna. The British Army, having accomplished one of the most celebrated retreats recorded in modern history, repulsing the pursuing enemy in all his attacks, and having traversed two

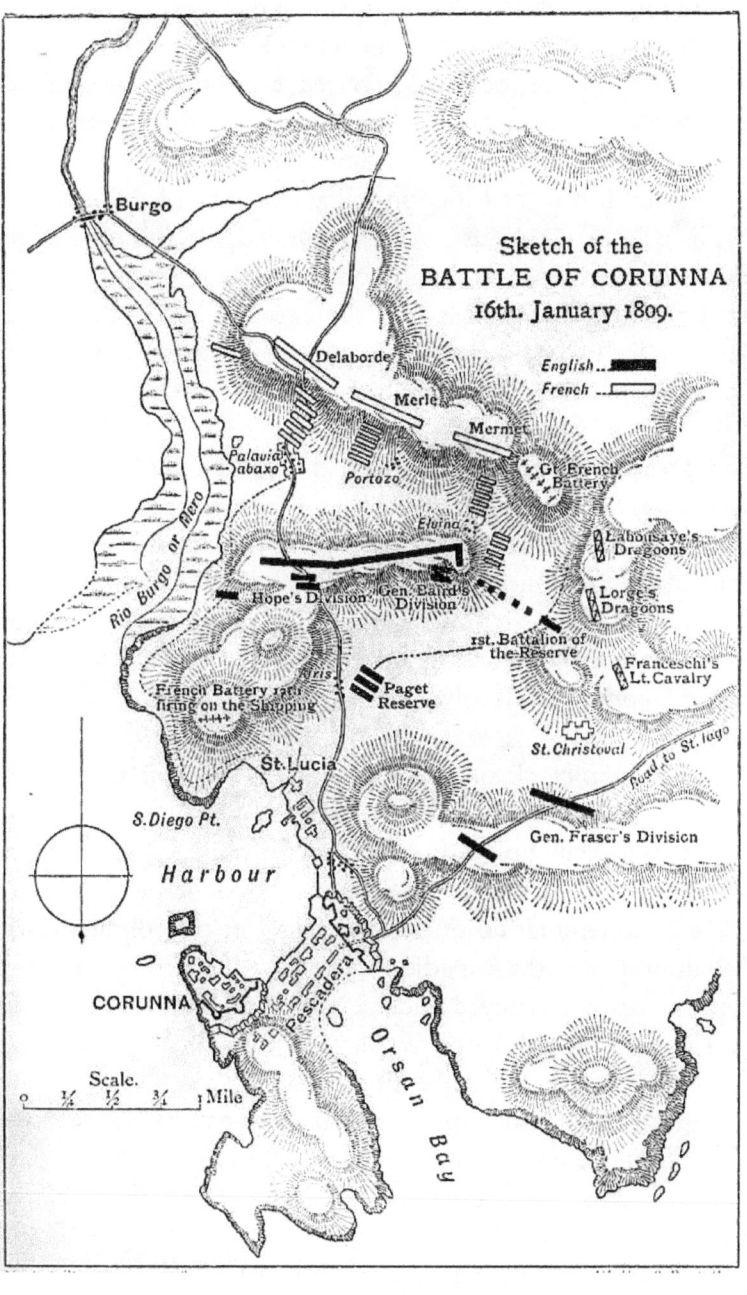

hundred and fifty miles of mountainous country under very disheartening circumstances, accompanied by severe privation, was not destined to embark for England without a battle.

The transports not having arrived, a position was occupied in advance of Corunna, and some sharp skirmishing ensued, in which four companies of the Seventy-First were warmly engaged, and lost several men in killed and wounded. Lieutenant William Lockwood was severely wounded. On this ground the Battle of Corunna was fought, on the 16th of January; but the Seventy-First, being placed on the extreme left of the British line, had little to do therein. The result of the action was glorious to the British Army, but was darkened by the loss of Lieut.-General Sir John Moore, who received a severe wound during the battle, and died at ten o'clock on the same night. His remains were wrapped in a military cloak, and interred in the Citadel of Corunna, over which Marshal Soult, with the true feeling of a soldier, erected a monument.

Lieut.-General Sir David Baird, who succeeded to the command upon Sir John Moore being wounded, was also wounded, and the command devolved upon Lieut.-General the Honourable John Hope.

At eight o'clock on the night of the 16th of January the troops quitted their position, leaving the piquets posted, and a few men to keep up the fires, and then marched into Corunna, where they embarked for England on the following day.

In commemoration of this battle, and of the conduct of the battalion during the expedition, the Seventy-First, in common with the army employed under Lieut.-General Sir John Moore, received the Royal Authority to bear the word "Corunna" on the regimental colour and appointments.

After the battalion had landed at Ramsgate, it was marched to Ashford in Kent, where it continued for some time, collecting the men, who from contrary winds were driven into different ports.

While at Ashford the battalion was brigaded with the Warwick militia and the Ninety-First regiment, under Brigadier-

General the Baron de Rottenburg. Great sickness prevailed at this station, and Surgeon James Evans and several of the soldiers died of typhus fever.

On the 20th of March 1809 the Royal Authority was granted for the Seventy-First to be formed into a light infantry regiment, when it was directed that the clothing, arming, and discipline should be the same in all respects as the Forty-Third, Fifty-Second, Sixty-Eighth, and Eighty-Fifth regiments.

The first battalion marched, on the 27th of April 1809, for Brabourne-Lees barracks, and was brigaded with the Sixty-Eighth and Eighty-Fifth Light Infantry regiments. Every exertion was here made to increase the strength and improve the discipline of the corps. In June the first battalion was increased by a large reinforcement, consisting of several officers and 311 non-commissioned officers and privates from the second battalion, which continued to be stationed in North Britain. Several volunteers from the militia were also received at this period.

Immense preparations had been made by the British Government to fit out the most formidable armament that had for a long time proceeded from England. The troops amounted to 40,000 men, commanded by Lieut.-General the Earl of Chatham; the naval portion consisted of thirty-nine ships of the line, thirty-six frigates, and numerous gunboats and bomb-vessels, and other small craft, under Admiral Sir Richard Strachan. The object of the expedition was to obtain possession of the islands at the mouth of the Scheldt, and to destroy the French ships in that river, with the docks and arsenals at Antwerp. The first battalion of the Seventy-First, towards the end of June, received orders to prepare for the above service, and marched, on the 28th and 29th of that month, in two divisions, encamping near Gosport.

On the 16th of July the battalion, consisting of three field officers, six captains, twenty-seven subalterns, five staff, forty-eight sergeants, and 974 drummers and rank and file, embarked at Portsmouth on board His Majesty's ships *Belleisle* and *Impérieuse*, and towards the end of the month sailed for the Downs.

The battalion was brigaded, under Brigadier-General the

Baron de Rottenburg, with the Sixty-Eighth and Eighty-Fifth Light Infantry, in the division commanded by Lieut.-General Alexander Mackenzie Fraser, and in the corps of Lieut.-General Sir Eyre Coote, K.B.

The expedition sailed from the Downs on the 28th of July, and having arrived off the Roompet Channel, preparations were made for landing; small craft to cover the landing were also sent in shore, and the light brigade, composed of the Sixty-Eighth, Seventy-First, and Eighty-Fifth Light Infantry, were landed under their fire. In an instant they were in contact with the enemy's sharpshooters, who fell back, skirmishing. Being pushed hard, four guns, with their equipment, and several prisoners were taken by two companies of the Seventy-First, under Captains George Sutherland and Henry Hall, and one company of the Eighty-Fifth regiment.

A battery and flagstaff on the coast were taken possession of by the tenth company of the Seventy-First, and in lieu of a flag a soldier's red jacket was hoisted on it.

This advance having succeeded at all points, and the enemy having fallen back on Flushing and Middleburg, the army was disembarked. The advance then dividing, proceeded by different routes. The Seventy-First moved by the sea dyke on a fort called Ter Veer, the situation and strength of which was not sufficiently known, an enemy's deserter having given but imperfect intelligence respecting it.

After nightfall the column continued to advance in perfect silence, with orders to attack the post with the bayonet, when, on a sudden, the advance-guard fell in with an enemy's party, who came out for the purpose of firing some houses which overlooked the works. The column following the advance-guard had entered an avenue or road leading to the fort, when the advance commenced the action with the enemy, who, retiring within the place, opened a tremendous fire from his works with artillery and musketry.

Some guns pointing down the road by which the battalion advanced did great execution, and the Seventy-First had Surgeon Charles Henry Quin killed, and about eighteen men killed and wounded. The column, after some firing, retired, and the place was the next day regularly invested by sea and land. It took three days to reduce it, when it capitulated, with its stores, and a garrison of 800 men.

Flushing having been invested on the 1st of August, the Seventy-First, after the surrender of Ter Veer, were ordered into the line of circumvallation, and placed on the extreme left, resting on the Scheldt. The preparations for the attack on the town having been completed, on the 13th a dreadful fire was opened from the batteries and bomb-vessels, and Congreve rockets having been thrown into the town, it was on fire in many places. The ships having joined in the attack, the enemy's fire gradually slackened, and at length ceased. A summons being sent in, a delay was demanded, but being rejected, the firing recommenced.

On the 14th of August one of the outworks was carried at the point of the bayonet by a party of detachments and two companies of the Seventy-First under Lieut.-Colonel Pack.

In this affair, Ensign Donald Sinclair, of the Seventy-First, was killed; Captain George Spottiswoode and a few men were wounded.

Flushing, with its garrison of 6,000 men, capitulated on the 15th of August, and the right gate was occupied by a detachment of 300 men of the first or Royal Scots, and the left gate by a detachment of similar strength of the Seventy-First under Major Arthur Jones. The naval arsenal, and some vessels of war which were on the stocks, fell into the hands of the British.

The Seventy-First shortly after proceeded to Middleburg, where the battalion remained for a few days, when it was ordered to occupy Ter Veer, of which place Lieut.-Colonel Pack was appointed *commandant*, and Lieutenant Henry Clements, of the Seventy-First, town major. The battalion remained doing duty in the garrison until this island, after destroying the works, &c., was finally evacuated on the 22nd of December.

On the 23rd of December the battalion embarked in transports, and sailed for England, after a service of five months in a very unhealthy climate, which cost the battalion the loss of the following officers and men.

	Officers	Sergeants, Drummers, & Rank and File.
Died on service	1	57
Killed	2	19
Died after return home	2	9
Total	5	85

In passing Cadsand, that fort opened a fire on the transports, one of which, having part of the Seventy-First on board, was struck by a round shot, which carried off Sergeant Steel's legs above the knees.

On the 25th of December the first battalion of the Seventy-First disembarked at Deal, and marched to Brabourne-Lees barracks, in Kent, where it was again brigaded with the Sixty-Eighth and Eighty-Fifth Light Infantry, and was occupied in putting itself in an efficient state for active service.

Upon the Seventy-First being made light infantry, they were permitted to retain such parts of the national dress as might not be inconsistent with their duties as a light corps. A correspondence on the subject took place between Lieut.-Colonel Pack and the adjutant-general in April 1810, and the following reply was received from headquarters.

Horse Guards, 12th April 1810.

Sir,

Having submitted to the commander-in-chief your letter of the 4th instant, I am directed to state, that there is no objection to the Seventy-First being denominated Highland Light Infantry Regiment, or to their retaining their pipes, and the Highland garb for the pipers; and that they will, of course, be permitted to wear caps according to the pattern which was lately approved and sealed by authority.

I have, &c.

(Signed)   William Wynyard,

                              Deputy Adjutant-General.
Lieut.-Colonel Pack,
71st Regiment

****

The bonnet cocked is the pattern cap to which allusion is made in the above letter. This was in accordance with Lieut.-Colonel Pack's application; and with respect to retaining the pipes, and dressing the pipers in the Highland garb, he added, "It cannot be forgotten how these pipes were obtained, and how constantly the regiment has upheld its title to them. These are the honourable characteristics which must preserve to future times the precious remains of the old corps, and of which I feel confident His Majesty will never have reason to deprive the Seventy-First regiment."

****

On the 8th of May 1810 the first battalion marched to Deal barracks, where every exertion was continued to render it fit for active service. Here the battalion was deprived of the services of Lieut.-Colonel Pack, who was appointed a brigadier in the Portuguese Army under Marshal William Carr Beresford, afterwards General the Viscount Beresford.

Nothing of moment occurred until the early part of September, when the battalion received orders to hold six companies in readiness for foreign service. They were prepared accordingly by drafting into them, from the companies which were to remain at home, the most effective officers and men, several not having recovered from the Walcheren fever.

The following were the companies selected and completed for foreign service, namely:—

    1st, or Capt. McIntyre's,
    2nd, or "   Hall's,
    3rd, or "   Adamson's,
    4th, or "   Walker's,
    6th, or "   Spottiswoode's,
    10th, or "   Lewis Grant's.

They consisted of two field officers, six captains, fifteen lieutenants, seven ensigns, four staff, thirty-eight sergeants, twelve drummers, and six hundred and three rank and file.

On the 14th of September the above companies embarked in the Downs on board the *Melpomene* and *St. Fiorenzo* frigates; three companies, with the staff, and Brevet Lieut.-Colonel Nathaniel Levett Peacocke, on board the former; the remaining three companies, under Brevet Lieut.-Colonel Thomas Reynell, afterwards colonel of the regiment, on board the latter. They sailed on the following day for Lisbon, and entered the Tagus on the 25th of September, after a short and pleasant passage. The companies were disembarked on the following day, and quartered in the San Benito and Espirito Santo convents.

The greatest exertions were made to complete the companies in field equipment, bat-mules, &c., which being effected, the detachment marched from Lisbon on the 2nd of October to Mafra, where it was shortly afterwards joined by Lieut.-Colonel the Honourable Henry Cadogan, who assumed the command, and Lieut.-Colonel Peacocke returned to the second battalion in North Britain.

The detachment being ordered to join the army under Lieut.-General Viscount Wellington, then retreating before Marshal Massena, Prince of Essling, marched from Mafra on the 8th of October, and on the 10th of that month effected the junction at Sobral, where it was brigaded with the Fiftieth and Ninety-Second regiments under Major-General Sir William Erskine, in the first division under Lieut.-General Sir Brent Spencer, K.B.

The army having retired into a position in the rear of Sobral, that place was occupied by the Seventy-First, having for its support the Fiftieth and Ninety-Second regiments and Major-General Alan Cameron's brigade. On the 12th of October the piquets were violently attacked by the enemy's advance, and retired skirmishing. In the meantime, the place was ordered to be evacuated, and the piquets having joined, the Seventy-First took up a position on the outside, within musket-shot of the town. In this affair the detachment had eight men killed, and thirty-four wounded.

In this position the Seventy-First continued, when on the 14th of October they were again attacked with the greatest impetuosity, and charged with the bayonet. The enemy was completely repulsed, with very considerable loss in killed and wounded, being chased to the spot from which he made the attack. Both parties resumed their original position.

In Viscount Wellington's despatch reporting this affair, the names of Lieut.-Colonel the Honourable Henry Cadogan, commanding the Seventy-First, and that of Brevet Lieut.-Colonel Thomas Reynell, were particularly mentioned.

A soldier of the sixth company, named John Rea, behaved on this occasion in the most gallant manner, and particularly distinguished himself, for which he received a silver medal, with the following inscription:

To John Rea, for his exemplary courage and good conduct as a soldier at Sobral, 14th October 1810.

On the 15th of October the Seventy-First were ordered to withdraw into the position at Zibriera, which was a continuation of the lines of Torres Vedras. In this celebrated position, which bid defiance to the French Army, the troops were constantly on the alert, and occupied in rendering it as strong as circumstances would admit, and in observing the motions of the enemy.

Marshal Massena did not think proper to attack the British Army in this stronghold, and occupied his time in reconnoissances and demonstrations, until compelled, through want of provisions, and consequent sickness of his troops, to abandon his designs, and retire to a position in his rear. This object he finally effected in a masterly manner in the night between the 14th and 15th of November, followed by the allied forces. Both armies thus evacuated positions on which the attention of Europe had been fixed, and which they had occupied for a month in the presence of each other.

The division in which the six companies of the Seventy-First were placed advanced by the route of Alemquer, Cartaxo,

Atelaya, and Almoster, and halted in and about the latter place from the 20th to the 26th of November inclusive. The enemy in the meantime retired to an extremely strong position at and in the vicinity of Santarem, where Marshal Massena halted, although threatened by Viscount Wellington, who, after some manoeuvring, took up a position immediately in the enemy's front, having his head-quarters at Cartaxo, and the different corps of the army cantoned in the villages. The brigade to which the Seventy-First belonged occupied Alquintrinha.

At this place the Seventy-First remained in quarters until March 1811, at which period the army, having been reinforced, was about to resume the offensive, when the enemy retired during the night of the 5th of March, taking the same road, through Estremadura, by which he entered Portugal. (The remaining four companies of the first battalion of the Seventy-First regiment arrived in the Peninsula in the course of the year 1811, namely, two companies in March, and two in July 1811.)

The British Army accordingly advanced in pursuit of Marshal Massena, and the brigade in which was the Seventy-First accompanied it, moving by Redinha, Miranda de Corvo, and Saryedes, passing the Coa, a little above Sabugal, upon the 5th of April, and on the 9th arrived at Albergaria, a small town on the frontiers of Spain. The Seventy-First remained in Albergaria until the 2nd of May, when the enemy, having been strongly reinforced, moved from Salamanca, and on that day crossed the frontier with a large convoy of provisions for Almeida, then closely invested by the Portuguese forces under Brigadier-General Pack.

In consequence of this movement, the Allied Army broke up its cantonments on the Azava, and formed in order of battle upon the high ground behind the Duas Casas, the left extending to the high road to Almeida which crossed the river by a ford near Fort Conception, and the right keeping up a communication with the bridge at Sabugal; opposite the centre, the village of Fuentes d'Onor was strongly occupied by light infantry.

Upon the 3rd of May the French took post on the opposite

side of the valley of the Duas Casas, their left fronting Fuentes d'Onor, and their right extending about two miles and a half to Alameda. In the afternoon of the 3rd of May they attacked Fuentes d'Onor with much vigour. That post was defended with the greatest bravery until the light companies, being worn out and harassed by repeated attacks, were obliged to retire, and the enemy possessed himself of the lower part of the village.

The Seventy-First were now ordered up to support, and, commanded by Lieut.-Colonel the Honourable Henry Cadogan, charged the enemy through the village and across the Duas Casas, taking ten officers and about, a hundred men prisoners. The corps retained its conquest that night and the whole of the next day, but upon Sunday the 5th of May, the French having succeeded in turning some troops to the immediate right, were obliged to give way; having been immediately supported by the Seventy-Fourth and Eight-Eighth regiments, they again advanced, took possession of and retained the village until the conclusion of the action.

A struggle of such duration could not be carried on without great loss, and the Seventy-First suffered severely. They went into action about 320 strong, and lost nearly one half of their number in killed and wounded.

The Seventy-First had Lieutenants John Consell, William Houston, and John Graham, and Ensign Donald John Kearns, together with four sergeants and twenty-two rank and file, killed.

Captains Peter Adamson and James McIntyre, Lieutenants William McCraw, Humphrey Fox, and Robert Law (adjutant), Ensigns Charles Cox, John Vandeleur, and Carique Lewin, six sergeants, three buglers, and one hundred rank and file, were wounded. Two officers, with several men, were taken prisoners.

In commemoration of the gallantry displayed in this prolonged action, the Seventy-First subsequently received the Royal Authority to bear the words "Fuentes d'Onor" on the regimental colour and appointments.

Viscount Wellington particularly mentioned the name of Lieut.-Colonel the Honourable Henry Cadogan in his despatch, and being highly gratified with the conduct of the Seventy-First on this occasion, directed that a non-commissioned officer should be selected for a commission. According to His Lordship's recommendation, Quartermaster-Sergeant William Gavin was shortly afterwards promoted to an ensigncy in the regiment.

The Seventy-First, upon the 14th, returned to their old quarters at Albergaria, and remained there until the 26th of May, when the brigade was ordered to the Alemtejo frontier, as a reinforcement to Marshal Sir William Beresford's army, at this time besieging Badajoz, and threatened by the advance of Marshal Soult from the south of Spain. (Major General William Carr Beresford, marshal in the Portuguese service, was appointed a Knight of the Bath on the 16th of October 1810.)

On the 15th of May 1811, the second battalion embarked at Leith for South Britain, arrived at Ramsgate on the 23rd of that month, and remained stationed in England for nearly two years.

The first battalion, upon its route southward, crossed the Tagus on the 31st of May, and arrived near Albuhera on the 14th of June, having passed through Portalegre, Aronches, Campo Mayor, and Talavera Real.

The sanguinary Battle of Albuhera, fought on the 16th of May, had obliged Marshal Soult to retire previously to the arrival of the reinforcement, which being considered no longer necessary, the battalion retired to Elvas, where it remained two days; the battalion again moved to Toro de Moro on the 19th of June, where it remained for a month. At this encampment a detachment of 350 men, with a proportion of officers, joined from the second battalion then stationed at Deal.

About this period the first battalion became a part of the army under Lieut.-General Rowland (afterwards Viscount) Hill. The junction of the armies of Marshals Marmont and Soult having obliged Viscount Wellington to raise the siege of Badajoz, which had been resumed after the Battle of Albuhera, the battalion, in co-operation with His Lordship's retrograde movement, retired to Borba on the 20th of July. Here it remained until the 1st of September, when it moved to Portalegre, and thence marched to Castello de Vido on the 4th of October.

A detachment from Marshal Soult's army under General Girard having been collecting contributions in Spanish Estremadura, Lieut.-General Rowland Hill, with a view of putting a stop to his movements, broke up his cantonments at Portalegre upon the 22nd of October, proceeding by Albuquerque and Malpartida. On the 27th, when within a moderate march of the enemy at Arroyo-del-Molinos, Lieut.-General Hill halted his troops, and, at night, breaking up his bivouac, made a flank movement close to the road by which the French intended to march on the following morning.

In that position he awaited the approach of day, when, on the 28th of October, the British marched directly on the rear of the town with such celerity that the cavalry piquets were rushed upon before they had time to mount. The French main body, though in the act of riding out, had so little intimation of danger that the officers and men were surrounded before their formation was effected, and to seek safety they individually dispersed. Many of them were killed, and about 1,400 were taken prisoners. All the enemy's artillery and baggage were captured. General Brun and Colonel the Prince of Aremberg, together with several other officers, were among the prisoners.

In this brilliant affair the Seventy-First was one of the three corps that advanced through the centre of the town, and were, therefore, principally engaged; but the enemy, from his complete surprise, being unable to make a combined resistance, the British sustained but trifling loss.

The battalion subsequently returned to Portalegre, where it arrived early in November. Viscount Wellington having made preparations for the recapture of Ciudad Rodrigo, concentrated the main body of the army in that neighbourhood, and the troops under Lieut.-General Hill were therefore ordered to divert the enemy's attention in the south.

The first battalion of the Seventy-First remained at Portalegre until the 25th of December, when the brigade moved into Estremadura for the purpose of expelling the French, who were ravaging the country. After the performance of this duty, the battalion returned to its former quarters at Portalegre in February 1812.

Upon the 19th of March 1812, the battalion moved northward to Castello Branco, where it remained for about a week, and afterwards returned for the last time to Portalegre.

The Earl of Wellington having made arrangements for the third siege of Badajoz, Lieutenant-General Sir Rowland Hill's corps was destined to cover his movements, and with that view proceeded on the 21st of March towards Merida, and afterwards to Don Benito, where the troops remained for a few days; but upon the approach of Marshal Soult with a large army, with the intention of raising the siege, Lieut.-General Hill retired upon Albuhera, through Arroyo de San Servan and Talavera Real. (Lieut.-General Rowland Hill was appointed a Knight of the Order of the Bath on the 22nd of February 1812.)

Badajoz having been assaulted and carried by the troops under the Earl of Wellington on the night of the 6th of April, after a sanguinary conflict, the movement of Marshal Soult was rendered nugatory, and the troops under his orders retired into Andalusia.

Marshal Marmont having, during the progress of the siege, penetrated into the province of Beira, and threatened Ciudad Rodrigo and Almeida, the Earl of Wellington, after the fall of Badajoz, crossed the Tagus, leaving Sir Rowland Hill's force to watch Marshal Soult, which took post at Almendralejos for that purpose.

The battalion was stationed at this town from the 13th of April until the 11th of May. It having then become expedient to render the communications between the French Armies on the north and south of the Tagus as precarious as possible, by the destruction of the bridge of boats at Almaraz, the corps under Lieut.-General Sir Rowland Hill, being the most disposable and convenient force, was accordingly ordered on this important service.

The French, feeling the importance of this bridge to their

mutual strength and security, had surrounded it on both sides of the river with formidable enclosed works, having in the interior of them casemated and loop-holed towers. The troops appointed for these strong works, consequently, anticipated an arduous struggle.

Upon the 12th of May the corps broke up from Almendralejos, and marching by Truxillo and Jaraicejo, reached on the 18th of that month the *sierra*, five miles from Almaraz, on which stands the Castle of Mirabete. This post was so strongly fortified that it blocked up the only road to Almaraz for the passage of artillery, which was considered by the enemy absolutely necessary for the destruction of the works. Sir Rowland Hill thought otherwise; and ascertaining that infantry could cross the *sierra* by a track through Roman Gordo, he left his artillery, and descended at night with a column of 2,000 men.

The leading company arrived at dawn of day close to the principal fort, built on a height a few hundred yards in front of the *tête-de-pont*; but such were the difficulties of the road that a considerable time elapsed before the rear closed, during which the troops were fortunately sheltered by a ravine, unseen by the enemy.

On the 19th of May the Fiftieth regiment and the left wing of the Seventy-First, having been provided with ladders, were appointed to escalade the works of Fort Napoleon, supported by the right wing of the Seventy-First, and the Ninety-Second regiment.

From a feint made upon Mirabete, the French were aware that an enemy was in the neighbourhood. The garrison was on the alert; immediately opened a heavy fire, and vigorously resisted the efforts made to push up the scarp; but the moment the first men gained a footing on the parapet the enemy took to flight. The whole of this brilliant affair was completed in the short space of fifteen minutes, and with little loss.

The Seventy-First had Captain Lewis Grant, with one sergeant and seven rank and file, killed; Lieutenants William Lockwood and Donald Ross, three sergeants, and twenty-nine rank and file were wounded.

The names of thirty-six non-commissioned officers and soldiers of the Seventy-First were inserted in regimental orders for conspicuous bravery upon this occasion, and the Royal Authority was subsequently granted for the word "Almaraz" to be borne on the regimental colour and appointments. (When Lieut.-General Sir Rowland Hill was created a Peer in May 1814, his title was connected with the gallant affair above recorded, as he was styled Baron Hill of Almaraz, and of Hawkstone, in the county of Salop.)

The bridge and works in the neighbourhood of Almaraz having been completely destroyed, the Seventy-First returned to Truxillo, where they remained a few days, then moved to Merida, and afterwards to Almendralejos. Lieut.-General Sir Rowland Hill's force having received orders to make a diversion in the south, while the main army was moving northward on Salamanca, the battalion again moved from Almendralejos to the borders of Andalusia, through Llerena. On this march the advanced parties of cavalry were constantly skirmishing with the enemy, but the Seventy-First were not engaged.

From Llerena the battalion returned to Zafra, where, after a short halt, it proceeded to Villa Franca, and finally to Don Benito. In these marches through Estremadura the weather was oppressively hot, and, joined to the clouds of dust raised by the troops, was so fatiguing that it was considered expedient at one time to move by night, and thus these inconveniences were alleviated.

While the force under Lieut.-General Sir Rowland Hill had been thus employed, the Allied Army under the Earl of Wellington had gained a victory on the 22nd of July over the French at Salamanca, for which he was advanced to the dignity of marquis.

From Don Benito the battalion moved upon the 13th of September, and passing through Truxillo, Talavera, and Toledo, arrived at Aranjuez upon the 1st of October, from which place, after a halt of three weeks, it moved to Ponte Duenna, further up the Tagus.

The sudden approach of the united armies of Marshals Soult and Suchet rendered a speedy retreat necessary, and the division accordingly retired from Ponte Duenna in the night of the 28th of October, moving to form a junction with the army of the Marquis of Wellington, who had now relinquished the siege of Burgos. Near Madrid the division halted for a short period, when, being joined by the garrison of that city, the troops retired leisurely by the Guadarama Pass on Alba de Tormes. This town the Seventy-First occupied from the 7th to the 13th of November, and during that period sustained a loss in action with the enemy of one sergeant and six rank and file killed; one bugler and five rank and file wounded.

The army having received orders to retire on Portugal, the battalion abandoned this post, arriving at Coria upon the 1st of December, where the retreat terminated. In this quarter the Seventy-First continued until the 13th of December, at which time they were pushed forward to Puerto de Bannos, where they were joined by a draft of 150 men from the second battalion.

While stationed at this post, an attempt was made, in February 1813, by the French, to surprise Bejar, then occupied by the Fiftieth regiment. The Seventy-First were ordered forward to support, but previously to their arrival that brave regiment had driven back the enemy, and completely foiled his efforts.

On the 18th of March 1813, the second battalion of the Seventy-First embarked at Gravesend for North Britain, and arrived at Leith on the 23rd of that month.

Upon the 5th of April the Seventy-First changed quarters with the Fiftieth regiment, and continued to occupy Bejar until the 21st of May, at which period the army broke up from its winter cantonments for active operations. The battalion on its advance moved by Salamanca and Toro, and encamped at La Puebla on the 20th of June, the evening before the memorable Battle of Vittoria.

Upon the morning of the 21st of June, the two armies being in position, the Seventy-First were ordered to ascend the heights of La Puebla, to support the Spanish forces under General Morillo. They accordingly advanced in open column, and having formed line, were immediately hotly engaged with the enemy, and upon this occasion suffered an irreparable loss in the fall of their Commanding Officer the Honourable Colonel Henry Cadogan, who fell mortally wounded while leading his men to the charge, and being unable to accompany the battalion, requested to be carried to a neighbouring eminence, from which he might take a last farewell of them and the field. In his dying moments he earnestly inquired if the French were beaten; and on being told by an officer of the regiment, who stood by supporting him, that they had given way at all points, he ejaculated, "God bless my brave countrymen" and immediately expired. (The officers of the Seventy-First regiment, to mark their admiration and esteem for this distinguished officer, had a monument erected to his memory.)

While recording the deep sense of sorrow which the Seventy-First experienced in the demise of a commanding officer who had so often fought at their head, and whose devoted gallantry had so frequently called forth their admiration, it is but a meet tribute to the memory of that brave spirit to extract from the despatch of the Marquis of Wellington the following expressions of His Lordship's regret at his loss:

"And I am concerned to report that the Honourable Lieut.-Colonel Cadogan has died of a wound which he received. In him His Majesty has lost an officer of great zeal and tried gallantry, who had already acquired the respect and regard of the whole profession, and of whom it might be expected, that if he had lived he would have rendered the most important services to his country."

After the fall of the lieut.-colonel, the Seventy-First continued advancing, and driving the enemy from the heights, until the force which was opposed to them became so unequal, and the loss of the battalion so severe, that it was obliged to retire upon the remainder of the brigade. In the performance of this arduous duty the battalion suffered very severely, having had one field officer, one captain, two lieutenants, six sergeants, one bugler, and seventy-eight rank and file killed; one field officer, three captains, seven lieutenants, thirteen sergeants, two buglers, and two hundred and fifty-five rank and file were wounded.

The officers killed were Colonel the Honourable Henry Cadogan, Captain Henry Hall, Lieutenants Humphrey Fox and Colin Mackenzie. Those wounded were Brevet Lieut.-Colonel Charles Cother, Captains Samuel Reed, Joseph Thomas Pidgeon, William Alexander Grant, Lieutenants Alexander Duff, Loftus Richards, John McIntyre, Charles Cox, William Torriano, Norman Campbell, and Thomas Commeline.

On this occasion the French suffered a great loss of men, together with all their artillery, baggage, and stores. King Joseph, whose carriage and court equipage was seized, had barely time to escape on horseback. The defeat was the most complete that the French had sustained in the Peninsula. It was this victory which gained a baton for the Marquis of Wellington, who was appointed a field marshal. In a most flattering letter, the prince regent, in the name and behalf of His Majesty, thus conferred the honour:

> You have sent me among the trophies of your unrivalled fame the staff of a French marshal, and I send you in return that of England.

This was in allusion to the baton of Marshal Jourdan, which was taken by the Eighty-Seventh regiment at Vittoria.

The Seventy-First subsequently received the Royal Authority to bear the word "Vittoria" on the regimental colour and appointments, in commemoration of this signal victory.

When the Seventy-First paraded on the morning of the 22nd of June, the dreadful havoc made by the action of the preceding day became painfully manifest, and a universal gloom was thrown over all, at missing from their ranks nearly four hundred brave comrades who had been either killed or wounded on the heights of La Puebla.

The enemy, having been completely beaten at all points, was forced to retreat in confusion on Pampeluna, and the British

Army immediately followed in pursuit. The battalion in this advance arrived at Pampeluna on the 29th of June, and shortly afterwards followed, as part of Sir Rowland Hill's army, a large force of the enemy, who were retreating into France by the valley of Bastan. During this forward movement the Seventy-First had some skirmishing in the valley of Elizondo, but without loss. Upon the 8th of July the Seventy-First arrived at the heights of Maya, from whence, for the first time, they had the cheering prospect of beholding the Empire of France extended before them in all its fertile beauty. Joy was diffused through every heart; every trial and danger were forgotten while viewing this splendid and gratifying sight. Upon these heights the battalion was encamped until the 25th of July.

Marshal Soult having been selected by Napoleon for the command of the French Army in Spain, with the rank of "Lieutenant of the Emperor," that officer used the most active exertions for its reorganisation, and made immediate arrangements for forcing the British position in the Pyrenees. With this view he advanced in person with a large force against the right, stationed at Roncesvalles, and detached Count D'Erlon with about thirteen thousand men to attack the position of Maya.

The Count D'Erlon, upon the 25th of July, advanced against the right of the Maya heights, where the ridges of the mountains branched off towards his camp. The force at this point was not sufficient to resist such formidable numbers, and the reserve being posted at some distance to watch passes of importance, which could not be left wholly unguarded, was brought up by battalions as the pressure increased.

The intrepidity with which these attacks were met, and the obstinate bravery with which every inch of ground was disputed, were obliged at last to yield to overwhelming numbers; but although the troops were forced to retrograde, yet in their retreat they took advantage of every rising ground, and disputed it with the utmost tenacity. At the commencement of this attack a part of the first battalion of the Seventy-First regiment was detached to a neighbouring high peak, under the command of

Major William Fitzgerald of the Eighty-Second regiment, and was strengthened by a company of that gallant corps. Lieut.-General the Honourable Sir William Stewart, in his report to Lieut.-General Sir Rowland Hill, thus expressed himself respecting these men:

> I cannot too warmly praise the conduct of that field officer (Major Fitzgerald) and that of his brave detachment. They maintained the position to the last; and were compelled, from the want of ammunition, to impede the enemy's occupation of the rock by hurling stones at them.

In another part of this communication, the lieut.-general thus alluded to the Eighty-Second regiment and to the first brigade, which was composed of the Fiftieth, Seventy-First, and Ninety-Second regiments:

> I feel it my duty to recommend to your attention, and favourable report to the commander of the forces, the conduct and spirit of Colonel Grant, and of his brave corps, the Eighty-Second regiment; also, the whole of the first brigade, than which His Majesty's army possesses not men of more proved discipline and courage. The wounds of him, and every commanding officer in that brigade, were attended with circumstances of peculiar honour to each of them, and to those under their orders.

The following is a list of the killed and wounded in the action of the 25th of July, as nearly as could be ascertained: Three sergeants and fifty-four rank and file killed; six sergeants, one bugler, and seventy-six rank and file wounded.

The Seventy-First continued retiring until the 30th, when Lieut.-General Sir Rowland Hill took up a strong position beyond Lizasso. In this post they were attacked with much spirit by the enemy, who, at the same time, by manoeuvring on the left flank, rendered necessary a change of position to a range of heights near Eguaros, which all the efforts of the French failed to carry. Upon this occasion the Seventy-First were seriously engaged, and had one sergeant and twenty-three rank and file killed; two sergeants, one bugler, and thirty-three rank and file were wounded.

The enemy having been foiled in all the objects of his attacks, found it necessary, in his turn, to retreat, moving on the 31st of July by the pass of Dona Maria, where he left a strong corps in an excellent position. This force was immediately attacked by the columns of Lieut.-Generals Sir Rowland Hill and the Earl of Dalhousie, and dislodged, after a gallant resistance. In the action of this day the first brigade, consisting of the Fiftieth, Seventy-First, and Ninety-Second regiments, had the honour of bearing its share, and of distinguishing itself. The Seventy-First had one sergeant and twenty-nine rank and file killed; two sergeants and forty-five rank and file were wounded.

The battalion now returned to the heights of Maya, from whence, after a halt of a few days, it moved to Roncesvalles.

The Royal Authority was subsequently granted to the Seventy-First to bear the word "Pyrenees" on the regimental colour and appointments, in commemoration of the services of the first battalion in the actions of the 25th, 30th, and 31st of July, which have been designated the "Battles of the Pyrenees"

In these actions the Seventy-First had Lieutenant Alexander Duff killed; Major Maxwell Mackenzie, Captains Leslie Walker and Alexander Grant, Lieutenants Thomas Park, John Roberts, William Woolcombe, William Peacocke, and Anthony Pack wounded. The following "Morning Reports" of the 14th of June and 7th of August, the former being prior to the battle of Vittoria, and the latter a few days subsequent to the actions in the Pyrenees, will show how the ranks of the Seventy-First were thinned within a period of less than two months.

	Sergts.	Buglers.	Rank & File
14th June 1813, present & fit for duty	54	21	909
7th August 1813 Ditto	21	15	356
Decrease	33	6	553

For nearly three months the battalion was encamped on the heights of Roncesvalles, during which period St. Sebastian and Pampeluna were captured. The men were principally employed during this interval in the construction of block-houses and batteries, and the formation of roads for the artillery.

In the early part of the season the neighbouring heights of Altobispo were occupied weekly by the brigades of the division; but as the cold increased with the high winds, the piquets alone were appointed for this duty. Such was the inclemency of the weather, and natural advantages of this position, that it was scarcely thought that the enemy would attempt an attack. This opinion, however, was ill founded, as upon the night of the 11th of October an attempt was made by a strong party upon the advance, composed of fifteen men of the Seventy-First, under Sergeant James Ross. Instead of flinching from an unequal contest, this small band, relying upon the strength of the position, and being, moreover, favoured by the darkness, which concealed its strength, maintained its ground, and forced the enemy to retire. The bravery of this party called forth high encomiums from Lieut.-General the Honourable Sir William Stewart, commanding the division, and at his request the soldiers composing it were all presented with medals.

On the 8th of November the division was again in motion, for the purpose of entering the French territory; and on the 9th of that month, it bivouacked near the heights of Maya, where orders were received to march as light as possible. The heights were passed that night by moonlight, for the purpose of joining the grand army; but the march over bad roads was so fatiguing that when the brigade arrived in position on the Nivelle it was not called upon to take an active part in the glorious proceedings of the rest of the army on the 10th of November, in forcing the French from their fortified position on that river.

After the Battle of the Nivelle, the battalion marched in the direction of Cambo, on the Nive, where some smart skirmishing occurred, in which two men were killed, and four sergeants, one bugler, and forty-one rank and file wounded. When the French crossed to the right bank, the Seventy-First occupied part of the town of Cambo.

The battalion remained in Cambo for nearly a month, and was here joined by a detachment of four sergeants and eighty-two rank and file, under the command of Lieutenant Charles Henderson, from the second battalion, at this period stationed at Glasgow.

On the 9th of December the first battalion was engaged in the passage of the Nive. The left wing of the Seventy-First entered the river, supported by the fire of the right, and reached the opposite bank without experiencing any loss.

The enemy now retired within Bayonne, and the corps of Lieut. -General Sir Rowland Hill was established with its right on the Adour, the left above the Nive, and the centre at St. Pierre, across the high road to St. Jean Pied-de-Port.

In this disposition the second division, of which the Seventy-First formed part, was placed at St. Pierre. Marshal Soult having completely failed in an attempt which he made against the left of the army, moved with his whole force against Sir Rowland Hill's corps, with the expectation of overwhelming him before he could be supported.

The enemy came on with great boldness upon the 13th of December, and made vigorous efforts against the centre, which he repeatedly attacked; but at last, finding his most earnest endeavours fruitless, he drew off. In the action of this day the loss of the first battalion of the Seventy-First regiment was very severe, having been placed close to the main road, against which the French made such formidable and repeated attacks.

Brevet Lieut.-Colonel Maxwell Mackenzie, and Lieutenants William Campbell and Charles Henderson, together with two sergeants, one bugler, and twenty-three rank and file were killed. Captains Robert Barclay and William Alexander Grant, and Lieutenants John McIntyre and William Torriano, with thirty-seven rank and file, were wounded. In commemoration of these services, the Seventy-First subsequently received the Royal Authority to bear the word "Nive" on the regimental colour and appointments.

The battalion marched on the 19th of December to Urcuit, and to Urt upon the 28th of that month. A small piquet of the Seventy-First, under the command of Corporal Dogherty, here distinguished itself, by beating off an enemy's party of nearly treble its strength.

While stationed in this quarter, the companies were frequently engaged in skirmishes with the enemy, particularly at St. Hellette, heights of Garris, and St. Palais, in the month of January 1814.

In the beginning of February, the battalion marched from Urt, and during its advance had frequent skirmishes with the enemy's rearguard.

On the 26th of February the battalion was in action at Sauveterre, and upon the 27th had the honour of participating in the Battle of Orthes.

In commemoration of this victory the Seventy-First afterwards received the Royal Authority to bear the word "Orthes" on the regimental colour and appointments.

Two divisions of the French Army having retired to Aire, after the action of the 27th of February, Lieut.-General Sir Rowland Hill moved upon that town to dislodge them. Upon the 2nd of March the French were found strongly posted upon a ridge of hills, extending across the great road in front of the town, having their right on the Adour. The second division attacked them along the road, seconded by a Portuguese brigade, and drove them from their position, in gallant style. Lieutenant James Anderson and seventeen rank and file were killed; Lieutenant Henry Frederick Lockyer, one sergeant, and nineteen rank and file, were wounded.

A detachment from the second battalion, consisting of one captain, four subalterns, and a hundred and thirty-four rank and file, under the command of Major Arthur Jones, joined at Aire.

On the 25th of March part of the battalion was engaged in an affair at Tarbes, in which Lieutenant Robert Law was wounded, and upon the 10th of April was in position at Toulouse, where some of the companies were employed skirmishing, and sustained a loss of one sergeant and three rank and file killed; six rank and file were wounded.

During the night of the 11th of April, the French troops evacuated Toulouse, and a white flag was hoisted. On the following day the Marquis of Wellington entered the city, amidst the acclamations of the inhabitants. In the course of the afternoon of the 12th of April intelligence was received of the abdication of Napoleon, and had not the express been delayed on the journey by the French police the sacrifice of many valuable lives would have been prevented.

A disbelief in the truth of this intelligence occasioned much unnecessary bloodshed at Bayonne, the garrison of which made a desperate sortie on the 14th of April, and Lieutenant Sir John Hope (afterwards Earl of Hopetoun) was taken prisoner. Major-General Andrew Hay was killed, and Major-General Stopford was wounded.

A treaty of peace was established between Great Britain and France; Louis XVIII. was restored to the throne of France; and Napoleon Bonaparte was permitted to reside at Elba, the sovereignty of that island having been conceded to him by the allied powers.

The war being ended, the first battalion of the Seventy-First regiment marched from Toulouse to Blanchfort, where it was encamped for sixteen days, and afterwards proceeded to Pouillac, where it embarked on the 15th of July for England, on board of His Majesty's ship *Sultan*, of seventy-four guns.

In addition to the other distinctions acquired during the war in Spain, Portugal, and the south of France, the Seventy-First subsequently received the Royal Authority to bear the word "Peninsula" on the regimental colour and appointments.

The first battalion arrived at Cork on the 28th of July, and marched to Mallow, where it remained for a few days. On the 4th of August the battalion marched to Limerick, where Colonel Reynell assumed the command of it in December, and in which city it continued to be quartered during the remainder of the year.

The second battalion remained stationed in North Britain.

In January 1815, the first battalion of the Seventy-First regiment marched from Limerick to Cork, and embarked as part of an expedition under orders for North America. Peace having been concluded with the United States, and contrary winds having prevented the sailing of the vessels, the destination of the battalion was changed, and subsequent events occasioned its being employed against its former opponents. The tranquillity which Europe appeared to have gained by the splendid successes over the French in the Peninsula was again to be disturbed.

Napoleon, who had been accustomed to imperial sway, was naturally discontented with his small sovereignty of Elba. Besides, the correspondence kept up by him with his adherents in France gave him hopes of regaining his former power, which were, for a short time, fully realized. Napoleon Bonaparte landed at Cannes, in Provence, on the 1st of March 1815, with a small body of men, and on the 20th of that month entered Paris at the head of an army which had joined him on the road. This could not be matter of wonder, for the officers and soldiers had won their fame under his command, and gladly welcomed their former leader, under whom they probably expected to acquire fresh honours, which might cancel the memory of the defeats sustained in the Peninsula.

Louis XVIII., unable to stem the torrent, withdrew from Paris to Ghent, and Napoleon resumed his former dignity of Emperor of the French. This assumption the allied powers determined not to acknowledge, and resolved to deprive him of his sovereignty, and again restore the ancient dynasty.

The first battalion of the Seventy-First, in consequence of these occurrences, proceeded to the Downs, and was there transhipped into small craft, which conveyed it to Ostend, where it disembarked on the 22nd of April.

The battalion next proceeded to Ghent, and, after remaining there a week, marched to Leuze, between Ath and Tournay, and was subsequently placed in the light brigade with the first battalion of the Fifty-Second, six companies of the second and two companies of the third battalion of the Ninety-Fifth regiment (Rifles), under the command of Major-General Frederick Adam, in the division of Lieut.-General Sir Henry Clinton.

The strength of the brigade was as follows:

	Rank and File.
52nd regt. 1st bat.	997
71st do. do.	788
95th do. 2nd bat. Rifles	571
95th do. 3rd do. do.	185
Total	2,541

Brevet Colonel Reynell, afterwards Lieut.-General Sir Thomas Reynell, commanded the battalion at this period.

Napoleon resolved on attacking the Allies before then: forces had been fully collected, and by well-masked and admirably combined movements, a portion of his army was concentrated on the 14th of June between the Sambre and the Meuse.

On the morning of the 16th of June, as the battalion was proceeding to the usual exercising ground of the brigade at Leuze, it received orders for an immediate advance upon Nivelles, where it arrived late that night. On the same day Prince Blucher had been attacked at Ligny, and was forced to retreat to Wavre. The Duke of Wellington and a portion of his army had been also attacked at Quatre Bras by Marshal Ney, who, however, made no impression upon the British position.

In the course of the morning of the 17th of June, the Duke of Wellington made a retrograde movement upon Waterloo, in order to keep up his communication with the Prussians. At daybreak on the same morning, the first battalion of the Seventy-First retired, and broke up its position, with the rest of the Allied Army, on the plains in the neighbourhood of Waterloo, being situated to the left and rear of Hougomont.

The Seventy-First, with the rest of the army, bivouacked in position during the night of the 17th of June, drenched by the rain, which fell heavily. Upon the morning of the memorable 18th of June, the battalion stood in open column, and in this situation was exposed for some time to a heavy fire of artillery, but a judicious movement to a short distance alleviated in a great measure this annoyance. Line was next formed, and about two o'clock the battalion, with the rest of the brigade, advanced, met their opponents in position, charged, and instantly overthrew them.

A heavy fire now commenced upon the retreating enemy, but the *alignement* having been completely deranged by the impetuosity of the advance, Colonel Reynell, with his usual coolness, proceeded to restore order, and had just completed the dressing of the line when the French cavalry were seen advancing. Square was instantly formed, and the Seventy-First, with the rest of the brigade, sustained a charge from three regiments of French cavalry, namely, one of *cuirassiers*, one of *grenadiers-à-cheval*, and one of lancers.

The charge was made with the most obstinate bravery, but nothing could overcome the steadiness of the British infantry, and after a destructive loss, the French were forced to retire.

Previously to this advance, the square of the Seventy-First was struck by a round-shot, which killed or wounded an officer and eighteen men of the eighth company.

About seven o'clock in the evening the left wing of the battalion was formed in rear of the right, and, while thus placed, was, with the rest of the division, attacked by a column of the Imperial Guard. These troops were fresh, having been kept in reserve during the day. They were allowed to approach close without molestation, and the regiments throwing in a close and well-directed fire, they could not deploy, but broke, and retired in confusion.

The enemy having now exhausted all his efforts, the British, in their turn, advanced. The Seventy-First, in the first instance, suffered much from the fire of some guns that raked their front; these were soon silenced, and the battalion was afterwards left unmolested. In this advance the light brigade captured several guns. Night closed in fast, and the corps rested after this lengthened and sanguinary encounter, the pursuit of the discomfited enemy being committed to the Prussians, under Marshal Blucher, who had arrived on the field of battle.

The Seventy-First had Brevet Major Edmund L'Estrange (*aide-de-camp* to Major-General Sir Denis Pack, K.C.B.), and Ensign John Todd, killed. The following officers were wounded: the lieut.-colonel commanding the battalion, Colonel Thomas Reynell; Brevet Lieut.-Colonel Arthur Jones; Captains Samuel Reed, Donald Campbell, William Alexander Grant, James Henderson, and Brevet-Major Charles Johnstone; Lieutenants Joseph Barrallier, Robert Lind, John Roberts, James Coates, Robert Law, Carique Lewin, and Lieutenant and Adjutant William Anderson.

The number of sergeants, buglers, and rank and file killed amounted to twenty-nine; one hundred and sixty-six were wounded, and thirty-six died of their wounds.

Both Houses of Parliament, with the greatest enthusiasm, voted their thanks to the army "for its distinguished valour at Waterloo."

For the share which the battalion had in this glorious victory, the Seventy-First were permitted to bear, in common with the rest of the army engaged upon the 18th of June, the word "Waterloo" on the regimental colour and appointments.

The officers and men engaged were presented with silver medals by His Royal Highness the Prince Regent, and were allowed to reckon two years additional service.

The battalion, with the rest of the army, afterwards marched towards Paris, and entered that city on the 7th of July. The brigade encamped that day in the Champs Elysées, near the Place Louis Quinze, being the only British troops quartered within the barriers, and continued there until the beginning of November, when it proceeded to Versailles, and to Viarmes in December.

Meanwhile Louis XVIII. had entered Paris, and was again reinstated on the throne of his ancestors. Napoleon Bonaparte had surrendered to Captain Maitland, commanding the *Bellerophon* British ship of war, and the island of St. Helena having been fixed for his residence, he was conveyed thither with a few of his devoted followers.

On the 24th of December 1815, the second battalion of the Seventy-First was disbanded at Glasgow, the effective officers and men being transferred to the first battalion.

ALSO FROM LEONAUR
AVAILABLE IN SOFTCOVER OR HARDCOVER WITH DUST JACKET

THE 9TH—THE KING'S (LIVERPOOL REGIMENT) IN THE GREAT WAR 1914 - 1918 by *Enos H. G. Roberts*—Mersey to mud—war and Liverpool men.

THE GAMBARDIER by *Mark Severn*—The experiences of a battery of Heavy artillery on the Western Front during the First World War.

FROM MESSINES TO THIRD YPRES by *Thomas Floyd*—A personal account of the First World War on the Western front by a 2/5th Lancashire Fusilier.

THE IRISH GUARDS IN THE GREAT WAR - VOLUME 1 by *Rudyard Kipling*—Edited and Compiled from Their Diaries and Papers—The First Battalion.

THE IRISH GUARDS IN THE GREAT WAR - VOLUME 1 by *Rudyard Kipling*—Edited and Compiled from Their Diaries and Papers—The Second Battalion.

ARMOURED CARS IN EDEN by *K. Roosevelt*—An American President's son serving in Rolls Royce armoured cars with the British in Mesopatamia & with the American Artillery in France during the First World War.

CHASSEUR OF 1914 by *Marcel Dupont*—Experiences of the twilight of the French Light Cavalry by a young officer during the early battles of the great war in Europe.

TROOP HORSE & TRENCH by *R.A. Lloyd*—The experiences of a British Lifeguardsman of the household cavalry fighting on the western front during the First World War 1914-18.

THE EAST AFRICAN MOUNTED RIFLES by *C.J. Wilson*—Experiences of the campaign in the East African bush during the First World War.

THE LONG PATROL by *George Berrie*—A Novel of Light Horsemen from Gallipoli to the Palestine campaign of the First World War.

THE FIGHTING CAMELIERS by *Frank Reid*—The exploits of the Imperial Camel Corps in the desert and Palestine campaigns of the First World War.

STEEL CHARIOTS IN THE DESERT by *S. C. Rolls*—The first world war experiences of a Rolls Royce armoured car driver with the Duke of Westminster in Libya and in Arabia with T.E. Lawrence.

WITH THE IMPERIAL CAMEL CORPS IN THE GREAT WAR by *Geoffrey Inchbald*—The story of a serving officer with the British 2nd battalion against the Senussi and during the Palestine campaign.

AVAILABLE ONLINE AT **www.leonaur.com**
AND FROM ALL GOOD BOOK STORES

www.ingramcontent.com/pod-product-compliance
Lightning Source LLC
Chambersburg PA
CBHW031628160426
43196CB00006B/322